T0012817

How to Launch a New Church Site

HOW TO

Launch
a New
Church Site

Ten Questions Every Leader

(and Church Member)

Must Answer

Jess Rainer

THOM S. RAINER, SERIES EDITOR

TYNDALE
MOMENTUM®

A Tyndale nonfiction imprint

Visit Tyndale online at tyndale.com.

Visit Tyndale Momentum online at tyndalemomentum.com.

Tyndale, Tyndale's quill logo, *Tyndale Momentum*, and the Tyndale Momentum logo are registered trademarks of Tyndale House Ministries. Tyndale Momentum is a nonfiction imprint of Tyndale House Publishers, Carol Stream, Illinois.

How to Launch a New Church Site: Ten Questions Every Leader (and Church Member) Must Answer

Designed by Dean H. Renninger

Scripture quotations are taken from the *Holy Bible*, New Living Translation, copyright © 1996, 2004, 2015 by Tyndale House Foundation. Used by permission of Tyndale House Publishers, Carol Stream, Illinois 60188. All rights reserved.

For information about special discounts for bulk purchases, please contact Tyndale House Publishers at csresponse@tyndale.com, or call 1-855-277-9400.

Library of Congress Cataloging-in-Publication Data

A catalog record for this book is available from the Library of Congress.

ISBN 978-1-4964-7372-1

Printed in the United States of America

29	28	27	26	25	24	23
7	6	5	4	3	2	1

To Rachel.

My beautiful wife. My best friend.

There is no one else I would want to share my life with.

I'm forever on Team Rachel.

I love you.

To Canon, Harper, and Collins.

I love you.

I'm proud of you.

I'm so thankful to be your dad.

Contents

We Need More Churches

"Hey, Jess, do you have a minute?"

That question always gives me pause, because as a pastor, I know that whoever is asking needs more than a minute. But something was different about the question that day.

Three months before we were to launch a new church site, I was sitting at the large community table in a local coffee shop. Whenever I'm out for coffee, I try to pay attention to the people around me. I look for opportunities to engage in conversation. But on this particular day, I was focused on writing a sermon. I had my earphones on and my head down.

When I first sat down, I had noticed Jason, another regular at the coffee shop, seated at the other end of the table. Jason worked in IT, and we'd had many conversations in the past. Focused as I was on my work, I wasn't aware that he had gotten up and walked down to my end of the table. Seeing that I had my headphones on, he tapped me on the shoulder.

"Hey, Jess, do you have a minute?"

Taking off my headphones, I replied, "Sure. What's going on, Jason?"

What I hadn't noticed was that another gentleman had sat down across from Jason at the end of the table. I would soon find out that the two men had been in a deep, spiritual conversation.

"Jess, I know you're a pastor. I've been talking with Shane, and I think you can help him. Will you talk with him?"

"Absolutely." I put away my headphones, closed my book, and shut down my laptop.

When I joined Jason and Shane at their end of the table, Shane told me about his life's pain, uncertainty, and confusion. He didn't have much resilience left. Life had thrown him a series of curveballs that had brought him low.

Realizing that Shane's heart was in a place where the Holy Spirit was working, I listened carefully and expressed compassion for all the challenging events he had endured.

"Shane, do you know Jesus?" I asked.

"Well, I know *of* Jesus," Shane replied. "What do you mean?"

I spent the next thirty minutes sharing the gospel message of Jesus with Shane. Over rapidly cooling cups of coffee, we stopped everything so Shane could begin a new relationship with Jesus.

God used a young pastor that morning to bring a new believer into the Kingdom. But God can use anyone at any time for his purpose. Most often, he works through the local church. That's his plan for reaching the world with the gospel of Jesus. Thus, we need more churches. We need more church members like Jason. We need more stories like Shane's.

Churches Are Losing Ground

Here's a sobering reality about churches: They are losing ground in many communities at an increasing rate. There are several ways to evaluate the data.

Scenario 1: The church is growing, but at a slower rate than the surrounding community. On the surface, this doesn't seem so bad. At least the church is growing. But it still means the church is losing ground.

Scenario 2: The church is at equilibrium while the community is growing. This scenario is dangerous. Church leaders and members may feel that everything is fine. Most likely, the church is stable, maintaining status quo. But what's really happening is a slow death. Over time, members will begin to age out or will leave the church. The church will soon find itself in scenario 3.

Scenario 3: The church is declining. It doesn't matter what is happening in the rest of the community; the church is losing ground.

I believe two significant factors contribute to churches losing ground:

Factor 1: More and more people are identifying as Nones—that is, with no religion. From 2007 to 2014, there was an increase of 19.2 million US adults who no longer identify with any religion. In 2015, about 23 percent of the US population did not identify with any religion—and the numbers have been on the rise ever since.[1] Younger generations aren't carrying on the faith of the family. Several areas of the United States have seen the impact of this for years. With the rise of the Nones, cultural Christianity continues to die. But this isn't necessarily a bad thing.

Factor 2: Churches have lost their intentionality with outreach and evangelism. There is no shortage of evangelism statistics. There is also no shortage of reasons why churches are less evangelistic than fifty years ago.[2] The point remains: Churches are sharing the gospel less and less.

Here's the bottom line: We need more churches that are dedicated to sharing the hope of Jesus. We need more churches that focus on evangelism and the gospel. We need more churches that are burdened for their neighbors' souls. Churches are losing ground, but they don't have to.

A New Church Site Will Change Your Focus

If you've read any books or articles about starting a new church site, you've probably come across a quote from C. Peter Wagner. In his book *Church Planting for a Greater Harvest*, Wagner writes, "The single most effective evangelistic methodology under heaven is planting new churches."[3]

I believe Wagner's quote *can* be true—*if* evangelism is the focus of the new church. But it's easy to start a new church site without being evangelistic. A new church can be a magnet for transfer growth. We'll address the issue of transfer growth later; but in the meantime, there's one thing we can say with certainty: Starting a new church site will change your focus.

Most people in the pews aren't thinking about starting a new church site. It's just not on their radar. More likely, they're sitting comfortably and aren't looking to disrupt the status quo. Sadly, the desire to be comfortable is leading to the decline of many, many churches.

Starting a new church site forces people to look beyond the walls of the existing church. Instead of asking inwardly focused questions such as "How do we increase our Sunday morning attendance?" or "How do we increase giving?" we start asking forward-looking questions such as "How do we reach this generation for Christ?" and "How are people in our congregation being equipped to share the gospel?" When the focus shifts outward, so does the impact of the church. When that happens, growth will occur in two ways.

First, growth will occur at the new church site. This type of growth is not surprising. After all, everything that goes into starting a new church site focuses on a single goal: reaching the community. Why, then, do new church sites often fail? They stop focusing outwardly. It's amazing how quickly a new church's congregation can become comfortable and stop growing. There's a solution to that problem, which we'll get to later. But typically, in the beginning at least, growth will occur with a new church site.

Second, growth will occur at the existing (or sending) church site. I know, it seems counterintuitive. If we send out people to open a new church site, won't that decrease the attendance at the existing church site? Temporarily, yes. But overall, it shouldn't. That's because it takes an outward focus to effectively start a new church site, and that same outward focus will continue to draw new people to the originating church site. The existing church will likely be growing in the months leading up to the launch of the new church site, and that growth should continue after the launch as well.

Here's an example of how this works: First Church averages one hundred people at their Sunday morning worship service. As a reflection of their outward focus, they decide to start a new church site. Over the next year, as the congregation shares Jesus with their community in preparation for the new church site, attendance at First Church grows to 150 people. After planning and preparation, First Church launches East Church by sending twenty-five people out to the new location. First Church now averages 125 people, and East Church averages twenty-five, for a total of 150.

During that first year, East Church continues their outward focus and grows from twenty-five to fifty. First Church continues to reach their community as well and grows from 125 to 150. Now, First Church is averaging 150, and East Church is averaging fifty for a total of two hundred people.

The total church attendance went from one hundred to two hundred people in two years. Both church sites end up growing.

Any Church Can Fail

Please hear me clearly: Church growth isn't guaranteed just because you launched a new church site. Any church can fail. But new church sites often fail for the same reason existing churches fail: They lose their outward focus and stop evangelizing. Any church that focuses only internally will die a slow death. New church sites that focus internally will die a quick death.

What's the solution? Reach your surrounding community with the gospel of Jesus Christ.

The odds of church growth increase dramatically when church leaders and committed church members team up to do something dramatic for God's Kingdom, such as starting a new church site. Establishing and maintaining an outward focus can change a church's trajectory for generations. If any church can fail, why not fail while trying to reach the next generation for Christ? Overall, churches are losing ground. But that doesn't have to include *your* church. We need more churches to start new sites. We need more churches to change their focus.

You may not think of yourself as a leader, but leadership takes many forms. What's most important is to find ways to get actively involved in the mission of the church to reach people in your community. I cannot emphasize enough how important it is for committed church members to support the starting of new church sites—whether that support is through prayer, by encouraging your leaders, helping out financially, or simply pitching in wherever you can. When committed members get on board with the church's mission, there's no limit to what God can do through the church.

You Have More Capacity than You Might Realize

Six months before I met Shane in that coffee shop, I didn't know if I had it in me to start another church. I had been part of two church plants in the previous four years, and I was tired. I didn't know if I had any more capacity to start a third church. Most leaders who want to start a new church site ask themselves the same question: "Do I have enough in me to do this?" Even the thought of shifting the focus of your church outward may seem overwhelming.

Let me give you some encouragement. You have more capacity to start a new church site than you realize. The people in your church have more capacity than they realize. Your leadership team has more capacity than you realize. The reason most church leaders don't believe they have the capacity to start a new church site can be summed up in one word: *assumptions*.

I would be surprised if anyone would begin exploring the possibility of starting a new church site without *some* assumptions. Most church leaders have at least an idea of what it would take. And before they even get started, they might convince themselves that it's a hill too big to climb. Here are some common assumptions:

- "It would cost too much money to start a new site."
- "We don't have enough leaders to make it happen."
- "There's no way the people in our church would agree to do this."
- "The people in our church are too tired."
- "Our community doesn't want another church."
- "It will take too long to start a new site."
- "We can't start a new church because we don't know how."

If God is calling you and your church to start a new church site, you can do it. I want you to turn any negative assumptions you have into prayer requests. Write them down now. Ask God to provide the necessary resources. Ask God to raise up new leaders in the congregation. Ask God to start preparing the hearts of the people in your church. Ask God to show you the needs in your community. Ask God to give you the wisdom to take the next step—not every step at once; just the next one. Surrender your assumptions to God, and let him start shaping your heart.

Starting a new church site will *not* turn out exactly as you think. Ups and downs, quick pivots, and unexpected turns are all a part of the process. That's a good thing. God will take you where you need to go. It might take longer than you planned. It might cost more than you budgeted for. It might not result in as many people as you wanted. But that's okay. If God is determining the next steps—instead of you—he may be changing your definition of success, as well.

Before you move on to the rest of this book, I encourage you to stop and pray. Starting a new church site is not an easy endeavor. I ask you to commit yourself fully to what *God* wants for your church and for you. I encourage you to seek absolute clarity on God's direction. Allow him to remove the obstacles to starting a new church before you even begin the process. I encourage you to be utterly dependent on God. It's the only way you can successfully launch a new church site.

Starting a new church isn't easy, but it's a worthy endeavor and a *needed* endeavor. Churches are losing ground, and it's time to start turning the tide. We need more churches—more outwardly focused, community changing churches. Let's start the process of launching new church sites because the world needs to hear about the free gift of salvation and hope that comes from knowing Jesus.

1

Are You Sure You Want to Do This?

HERE'S MY ADVICE: Don't start a new church site.

"Wait a minute! You just told me we need more churches because churches are losing ground. And you told me I have the capacity to start a new church site. Why would you turn around and tell me *not* to start a new church site?"

That's a fair question. But I stand by my advice.

Don't start a new church site.

Okay, let me explain.

Starting a new church site will be one of the most challenging ministry assignments you ever undertake. When people ask me what it's like to start a new church, I typically respond, "It's the most exhausting ministry I've ever done, but also the most rewarding."

In all honesty, it will be more exhausting than rewarding during the first few years. There will be days when you just want to be done with it. You'll want to walk away. You'll want help, but help won't come. To put it simply, starting a new church site will be full of tough days. But that doesn't mean it isn't worth it.

I just want to paint an accurate picture before you start the process of establishing a new church site. It wouldn't be fair—to you or your church—if I didn't give you the straight scoop. Ten months down the road, I don't want you to be thinking, *No one told me it would be like this! What in the world were we thinking?*

I hope you realize that *realistic* does not mean *pessimistic*. Any worthwhile Kingdom work is bound to encounter opposition. And starting a new church site is major Kingdom work.

To be clear: I *want* you to want to start a new church site. But more important, I want you to know you are called by God to start a new church site. If this is not God's initiative, it will be a tough road.

That's putting it too lightly. If this is not God's initiative, if God is not in the process from the very beginning, it will be a dead-end street.

Here's the biggest question that you must answer before you start: "Is God calling you to start a new church site?"

If God has not called you to this, the church site will fail. You will fail. There's no way around it.

As I do my best to paint an accurate—and encouraging!—picture of what it takes to start a new church site, my prayer is that it will prepare you and inspire you for the journey.

So, one last time: *Are you sure you want to do this?*

What's Your Motivation?

Discerning God's calling takes time. It's not a clear-cut process. Because of that, some leaders will use outside circumstances to influence what they believe is their internal calling. Unfortunately, these mixed motivations will set a new church site on a difficult path. Here are some outside circumstances that can confuse an inner calling:

- *You're unhappy where you are.* Unhappiness with a current situation is what often leads people to think about starting a new church site. It's the typical "the grass is always greener" scenario.
- *You're frustrated with your local church.* Frustration can be found in a pastor, a staff member, or a layperson. Frustration with the direction or vision of the local church (or the lack thereof) isn't a sufficient reason to start a new church site.
- *You think you should be in church leadership.* This mindset isn't necessarily wrong. The motivation to lead is needed for a new church site. But if you only want to start a new church site because you think you should be the leader, then your priorities may be misaligned.
- *You've been hurt.* Hurt causes us to react in different ways. Being hurt can't be the motivation for starting a new church site.
- *You think it would be cool to start a new church.* The pendulum often swings between starting new churches and revitalizing old churches. Depending on the pendulum's current position, there may be a certain emphasis on starting something new. Church planting looks cool. Don't be fooled; it's not as cool as you think.

What is the right motivation? What is the proper calling? Ultimately that's between you, your family, and God. There are two soul-searching questions to ask yourself. I call them soul-searching because they require some reflection. Your answers must be gut-level honest.

1. *Why are you starting a new church site?* This first question seems obvious. If you don't know why, you shouldn't be doing it. What are your motivation and calling? What makes your blood pump when you think about starting a new church site? How fueled are you to reach the unchurched and dechurched? Launching a new church site is more than just starting a new organization. It's Kingdom work. And it should motivate you.

2. *For whom are you starting the new church site?* In all my assessments and preparation as a church planter, no one ever asked me this question. But it's a good one. If we have improper motives for starting a new church site, it's hard to say we're doing it at God's initiative. If you're frustrated in your current situation, are you wanting to start a new church site to spite someone? If you're doing it because you think it sounds cool, does your motivation have more to do with impressing others? If you've been hurt by a previous church, are you starting a new site more for yourself than for God? Go into the corners of your heart and ask yourself, *For whom am I doing this?* If you come up with anything other than God, the gospel, and God's Kingdom, I suggest you pause and discern your calling.

Discern Your Calling

How do you know whether God is calling you to start a new church site? Potential church planters must spend a lot of time working through their calling from God. They may spend hours, days, and even weeks rooting out all the potential negative motivations for starting a church. It's a process. Some organizations will spend weeks evaluating a potential leader for a new church site. They are looking for clues to uncover the more honest, more profound answers. They know that leaders of a new church site must be vetted, and even challenged, in their calling. If you can be honest with yourself, you can start this process independently—but that doesn't mean you go it alone. If God is in it, he will bring trusted people around you to confirm his calling. Here are seven ways to begin discerning your calling:

1. *Pray.* Too often overlooked or neglected, prayer is the cornerstone of pursuing our calling. Prayer means talking to God, yes; but just as important are *listening* and *waiting* for his guidance and direction.

2. *Read the Bible.* God's living and active Word speaks. Read your Bible and pay attention to what God reveals.

3. *Look for other ministry opportunities.* Spend time researching ministry opportunities that match your gifts, abilities, and interests. If you are a current church leader, look for other ministry opportunities that align with your congregation before looking at starting a new church site. If you can see your church pursuing other ministries, God may not be calling you to start a new church site.

4. *Understand the push and pull of God's moving.* A mentor of mine, Dr. Brad Waggoner, once told me, "God will often push you away from where you are and pull you to where he wants you to be." Both pieces will be in play when God calls.

5. *Talk with godly people you trust.* Have other godly people join you in praying about whether God is leading you to start a new church site.

6. *Talk with your family.* Early in my ministry years, I started feeling the tug to preach. I had been serving in support roles in a church plant for several years, but I felt God was nudging me to something new. I sought out preaching opportunities. I wanted to explore this possible new direction. I still wasn't quite sure what it meant. I had never before felt the calling or the desire to become a lead pastor. For years, I had told my wife that I didn't feel called to that role. But now, after several months of exploration, I asked my wife, "Do you think God could be calling me to be a lead pastor?" She softly but truthfully answered, "Not yet." At the time, it stung a little bit. But looking back, she was 100 percent correct. I wasn't ready to become a lead pastor. Years later, when the calling came up again, and I asked my wife for her perspective again, she responded with wisdom, "If you believe without a doubt that God is calling you, then I believe God is calling you." One month later, our congregation started the process of planting a third church—with me as the lead pastor. Listen to your family. Let them speak into your life and your calling. Don't lead your family into a ministry where God doesn't want you to be. It'll be painful for everyone.

7. *Pray more.* When seeking God's direction, you can never pray too much. Without God's calling and covering, a new church site won't succeed.

Recognize Your Wiring

God can use different types of people to start a new church site. It isn't one size fits all. If you've read books, blogs, or articles about starting a church, or have completed a personality assessment, it might seem as if the ideal profile is a dynamic, driven, and outspoken leader.

Some would say that an ENTJ or an ENFJ on the Myers-Briggs scale would be the best fit for starting a new church. On the DiSC personality assessment, it would equate to the "dominance" attribute. On the Enneagram, they might identify an 8 (Challenger) or a 3 (Achiever) as the best fit. What these different measures of personality type have in common is a strong "get it done" mindset.

The danger in narrowing the scope too much on who is best suited to start a new church site is that it limits who God can work through. I believe that God can use anyone to start a new church. When I was first assessed as a church planter, I didn't get the green light to become a leader. To be fair, I wasn't ready to be a lead church planter, but I was preparing to join a church planting team. Several years later, while serving in another church plant, someone told me I would *never* be a fit to be a lead church planter. Why? Because I didn't fit that person's mold exactly of what a church planter should be. A year later, I planted the church that I've now been pastoring for six years.

Though God can use anyone to start a new church site, it's safe to say that those who succeed will most likely share some common attributes and characteristics. Based on observation, I've found that successful church planters typically fall into one of two broad categories: *connectors* or *pioneers*. These two categories can encompass a variety of different personality types.

Connectors and pioneers are both primarily vision casters. They see where God is leading and ask others to join in the journey. The primary difference between the two is how they approach their calling. Pioneers focus on strategy, whereas connectors focus more on people. For example, if both were given the goal of creating a community event to share the gospel, the connectors would go person to person, describing the goal and asking people to jump on board to figure out how to reach the goal. The pioneers would take time to figure out how to reach the goal and then find the right individuals to help achieve the goal. In a church planting scenario, connectors typically draw people to relationships, whereas the pioneers are more apt to draw people to the strategy.

As you consider starting a new church site, you must recognize your wiring. Are you a *connector*, or are you a *pioneer*? Don't try to fit a mold; instead, understand who you are and how God made you. If you understand your leadership style, you can lead more effectively.

Five Crucial Leadership Characteristics

Whether you're more of a connector or a pioneer, you want to build your leadership team based on five characteristics that every effective leadership team must possess. The primary leader doesn't have to possess all five. In fact, it's rare for one person to be strong in all five areas. But as a group, your leadership team should exhibit all five characteristics. Let's briefly look at each.

1. *Vision.* Where is the church going? Where is God leading? A visionary communicates what the anticipated future looks like.
2. *Strategy.* How is the church going to accomplish the vision? A strategist creates a clear path forward on how to reach the vision.
3. *Execution.* Who is going to complete the strategy? An executor implements the strategy. This person is the "get things done" person.
4. *Multiplication.* Who will bring people together to reach the vision and complete the strategy? Leaders of a new church site must multiply themselves by involving

others in the church. Challenge your committed church members to rally others in the congregation to support the new initiative.

5. *Shepherding.* Who will take care of the people as they pursue the vision? A shepherd cares for, prays for, and loves the people of the church.

Why is it vital to have these five leadership characteristics on your team? Because the path forward isn't easy. A new church plant is both volatile and fragile. No two weeks will look the same in the first fifty-two weeks of starting a new church site.

Satan knows this about new churches. I firmly believe that he hates new churches because of their effectiveness in spreading the gospel. Let me paint one more part of this picture. It may be the most important thing to understand before you start a new church site.

Impending Spiritual Warfare

With the first church I helped plant, our team consisted of full-time and bivocational staff. With our crisscrossing schedules, we held our weekly staff meetings on Mondays at 6 a.m.

As you might imagine, our meetings weren't laced with an abundance of energy. But one particular staff meeting was different from the others. I could see it in the eyes of my teammates; we were spiritually wounded and exhausted.

Since starting the church, our team had gone through the deaths of family members, unexplained physical ailments, and marriages that were falling apart. At the same time, the church was growing rapidly. We had more than three hundred people in attendance and had even started the process of opening a second campus. On the outside, everything looked good. On the inside, the team was hurting. We had been fighting battles that very few people saw.

The attacks never stopped as we planted a second church and eventually a third that I served as lead pastor. The second church was full of unnecessary conflict, and my current church has gone through seasons of hardship that are clearly fueled by the enemy. I've spent more than a decade planting three churches, and the spiritual warfare has lasted just as long. Only recently have I begun to learn how to distinguish spiritual battles from the normal ups and downs of starting a new venture. Yes, we live in a fallen world where bad things sometimes just happen. But we must also be aware that Satan hates new churches, and he will do whatever he can to slow them down or stop them.

No one prepared me for the spiritual warfare that came with starting a new church site. I'm still learning, and I want you to be aware of what can happen. I also want you to know that God is victorious, and he will see you through any battles you may face. As Christ builds his church, we can be certain that "all the powers of hell will not conquer it" (Matthew 16:18).

Permission to Fail

There are a lot of definitions of success when it comes to starting a new church site. In the chapters to come, you'll be able to determine what success looks like for you. For now, I want to talk about failure. It's okay not to succeed. You have permission to fail at starting a new church site.

We can put so much pressure on ourselves to reach a certain level of success with a new church site that we can miss all the incredible ministry that happens along the way. I've talked with several church leaders over the years who either left or closed down a new church site. Their tone and demeanor often reflect failure.

But I always remind them of the good work that God did along the way.

"How many adults, students, and kids heard the gospel over the life of the new site?"

"How many people did you disciple?"

"How many baptisms did you celebrate?"

"How many people did you send on missions trips through the church?"

And I always ask this question last: "How many people came to Christ through the church?"

I believe that every new church site is worth the effort if even just one person comes to a saving relationship with Jesus Christ. Changing someone's eternal destiny is always worth it.

Experience has shown that most new churches will see a lot more than just one person come to a saving relationship with Jesus Christ. In fact, evangelistic ministry during the first three years of a new church site will often produce more than three times the number of conversions as a similar size church fifteen years old or more.[1] I'll take the first three years of ministry impact at a new church site over the previous ten years at an existing church, which is more likely to be "steeped in complacency and the status quo and . . . to resist needed change."[2] Even if a new church site fails within the first two years, if its leaders and members have reached into their community, I consider that church a success.

Is God calling you to start a new church site? If so, *run* after the calling and you will see God accomplish things you wouldn't even know to ask or think.

2

What Will Your Church Site Look Like?

Several years ago, I met with the leadership team of a dying church. They were without a pastor and were down to a handful of families. But they didn't want their church to die.

"Do you think people would come to church here?" they asked. "We've done some community events recently, and people showed up. They just don't come to church on Sundays."

These church members had read books on church revitalization and had talked with other church leaders. They wanted to know if their church could be vibrant again.

I was optimistic. It seemed they were motivated to change. At the time, I was in the process of planting a third church. In my previous experience, I had engaged with dying churches to see how we could partner with them to restore some vibrancy. If my previous experience was any indicator of success, this church was on the right track.

During the conversation, I passed along a quote that my brother Sam has repeated many times: "If God can save any *person*, he can save any *church*." It seemed to motivate them. And I was motivated as well. I thought perhaps God was calling me to help "replant" this church while continuing to develop our new church site.

We began the process with a series of leadership meetings. I started preaching at the church on Sunday mornings. And other outside leaders agreed to provide leadership to the dying church for a year to help them make the needed changes. All the pieces were in place. The conversations were going well.

We sat down for a church business meeting to map out the transition. We discussed high-level concepts and some minor details. That's when everything changed.

A man in the church raised his hand and asked, "We will have screens?"

At first, I was confused by the question. "I don't quite know what you're asking. Can you clarify what you mean?"

"Will we have those screens up there on stage with the words to the songs?" he elaborated.

What I should have said was, "There will be a lot of details we'll need to discuss and work out together along the way." But without even thinking, I just said, "Sure."

In my experience, screens were common, and I assumed he was thinking they would want them. But I was wrong. For this man, having screens meant the hymnals would go away, and therefore the hymns would go away—to be replaced by drums and electric guitars. In his mind, if we put up screens, church as he knew it would be gone forever.

That may not have been the only issue, but a week later, the church decided not to move forward with replanting.

Within a year, they closed their doors for good.

The point of the story is that everyone has their own ideas about what a church should be like. The answer to the question "What will our new church site look like?" can send you down several different paths.

Adopt, Foster, Plant, or Multi-Site

There are four possible ways to develop a new church site: *adopt, foster, plant,* or *multi-site*. Let's look at some quick definitions of these options:

- **ADOPT:** Adoption is when one congregation brings another congregation into their church family.[1]
- **FOSTER:** Fostering refers to a healthier church helping a less healthy church for a season. In the case of adoption, the arrangement is permanent. In fostering, the relationship is temporary.[2]
- **PLANT:** Church planting is when a church sends out a group of people to start an autonomous church.
- **MULTI-SITE:** Multi-site is similar to planting, except the new location remains under the umbrella of the sending (existing) church.

Which path is best for you? The answer can be determined by asking two questions:

1. Do you want to work with an existing church—that is, with another church in your area that might be in decline or in danger of closing?

2. Do you want the new church site to be autonomous—
   that is, not under the umbrella of your current church?

The questions are simple, but the process of getting the answers
may not be. So let's work through the questions together, using
the following grid.

	Work with an existing church? NO	Work with an existing church? YES
New church site autonomous? YES	planting	fostering
New church site autonomous? NO	multi-site	adoption

There is often a third question that pertains to adoption and fostering: "Where do I find an existing church?"

Simple answer: You don't.

Adoption and fostering cannot be forced or manipulated. This
is not like some mergers and acquisitions in the business world.
Adoption and fostering must be a work of the Holy Spirit—
bringing two congregations together to further the work of God's
Kingdom. These paths are slower and have a lot more moving
parts. If your desire is to start a new church site soon, I recommend
planting or multi-site. I would not look for adoption or fostering
opportunities. When adoption or fostering are forced, it can create
a lot of unnecessary pain.

If you feel that God is leading you toward the adoption or fostering route, I encourage you to set this book aside for a time and find other resources specific to those paths. Once you have the proper framework in place for adoption or fostering, come on back. Though this book is written mainly for church planting and multi-site expansion, there are a lot of great tools in later chapters that you can use.

So now that you've prayerfully considered the path that God is leading you to take, what's next?

If you are ready to follow the church planting or multi-site path, you must decide how much of your current church's DNA will go into the new church site.

The DNA Decision

When the gentleman asked the question about screens that ended up putting the brakes on a church adoption, the fundamental question he was asking was, "What will my church look and feel like after this is done?" In other words, "What will our DNA be like?" Here are some "genes" that make up the DNA of a church:

- worship style
- evangelistic emphasis
- intentional discipleship
- focus on prayer
- Sunday school and/or home groups
- expository or topical preaching
- committee driven or staff driven
- policies and procedures

When you start a new church site from an existing church, you must decide how much of the existing church's DNA will carry over to the new one. Why not 100 percent? Because no two church settings are exactly alike. Every church has its own context. Even if the new church is only a few miles down the road, you must allow room for that church to do what it needs to do to reach the people in that area.

For the multi-site path, I encourage you to choose either 80 percent or 20 percent of the existing church's DNA to carry over. If the new church site has 80 percent of the existing church's DNA, the two churches will look and feel very similar—in worship style, evangelistic emphasis, and so on. If the new church has 20 percent of the existing church's DNA, the new church will look very different and will most likely reach a different demographic. In that case, the existing church will take more of a supporting role than a guiding role. With the 20 percent DNA approach, the new church site has a greater chance of reaching a new set of people. But there will be more challenges as the existing church learns to adapt to the differences.

You must make an intentional decision about DNA at the outset. You don't need ambiguity as you start down the path. Trying to walk the tightrope when it comes to the culture and DNA of the new church site will only create problems later.

For the church planting option, I would let the new church develop at least 90 percent of its own DNA. The goal is for the new site to be autonomous. If the sending church tries to control too much, it only slows down the progress of the church plant. Anything less than 90 percent diminishes the church plant's chances of becoming self-sufficient.

The Facility Decision

A church must gather for worship. So the next question to answer is, "Where are we going to meet?" This question must be answered as early in the process as possible—for two reasons.

First, it can take much longer than you anticipate to find a suitable meeting place. The logistical needs for a church facility are unique. Many existing buildings are neither set up for a church nor easily altered to accommodate a church. The process takes time. Start early.

Second, people want to know where you're going to meet for worship. As soon as the word gets out that you are starting a new church site, I can (almost) promise you will hear these two questions repeatedly:

- What is the name of the church?
- Where are you going to meet?

Though it's not a deal breaker, it's good to have these two questions answered before you announce the launch of a new church site.

We'll talk about naming the church in the next chapter, so for now let's stay focused on the meeting place. Yes, I know the church is not a building. The church is the people. So why am I emphasizing the need for a facility? Because the unchurched and dechurched don't know what it means that "the church is not a building." If they're going to come to worship, they need to know the address.

Remember, the goal of starting a new church is to reach new people for Jesus. You'll have plenty of time to overcome the knowledge gap and define for people exactly what the church is, but when you're launching a new site, there is an opportunity cost in everything you do. I strongly recommend that you keep the communication simple and outward focused. If this is a big issue for you, finding a Sunday-only location can help. We'll talk more about temporary versus permanent in a moment. For now, let's look at what goes into making the facility decision.

Geographical Location

The first—and most significant—step in finding a worship facility is *location*. Where you choose to plant your roots—shallow or deep—sets the tone and direction for the new church site.

Take time to study your community. Spend time praying for the community. Spend time *in* the community. Make sure you know the demographics and psychographics of the community.[3] Is God leading you to a particular demographic? If so, where is the best location for the church to reach them?

Is it your vision to be in a neighborhood? Or would a location near a major highway be better for a broader reach and easier access?

Geographical location is the most important facility decision you will make, so do it well. At the same time, give yourself some grace in the process. Chances might not be good that you will find a building at the exact pinpoint of your geographical location. Why? Because finding a suitable building can be difficult.

Building/Facility

The two primary options for a church facility are *permanent* or *temporary*. A temporary location may be an existing business or school that allows you to use their facilities on Sunday mornings only. Utilizing a temporary location typically means you will have to store your equipment off-site, most likely in a trailer that you can roll up to the door for setup. You will have to set up and tear down every Sunday. Examples of temporary locations include:

- local schools
- movie theaters
- public parks (this may require a permit from your city, and weather may also be a factor)
- homes (though this option may limit growth)

The most significant advantage of a temporary location is *cost*. Typically, you will pay a lot less to rent a Sunday-only location than a permanent location. The need for setup and teardown has its pros and cons. Initially, it can bring the people of the church together. It's almost like a weekly missions trip that can bond a church. On the other hand, setup and teardown can quickly lead to "volunteer fatigue."

The most significant disadvantage of a temporary location is not having control of the building. There's only so much you can do on Sunday mornings to make it look like a church. There are businesses out there that provide all the necessary equipment to make it happen (and make it look good), so that's something to keep in mind if you go that direction.[4]

Another disadvantage of a Sunday-only location is that your church may still need a central gathering place during the week, a place where people feel ownership. A quick solution is to find an office to rent. Having a place to host meetings and small groups can be of great benefit when you're using temporary space. Just make sure the cost of renting a temporary Sunday-only location plus the cost of an office doesn't get too expensive. It might be more advantageous at that point to rent a permanent building.

The other option is to find a permanent location, either rented or purchased. The obvious hurdle with a permanent location is cost. Purchasing a facility for a new church can be risky. The initial investment can take money from your ministry budget. Also, purchasing the wrong-size facility can hurt a new church site. If the church facility is too small, growth will be limited. If the church facility is too big, it will create a challenging atmosphere. Choosing a permanent location requires a lot of planning and forethought. It must be the right facility for what you believe your church will need.

Renting a permanent building can be a great option. It provides stability, visibility, and the ability to make the space your own. Some options for a permanent rental space include:

- office spaces
- retail spaces
- warehouse or industrial spaces

With renting a permanent location, you need to factor in the costs. Does the space need any structural changes for a church to meet there? If so, what modifications will you make? Will the space require any changes to comply with city codes and regulations? If so, what will need to be done, and at what cost? How long is the lease you will be required to sign? Are there any additional fees for renting the space, such as common area maintenance? Modifying the building in any way can take a lot more time and money than you think. But in the end, you control the space 24/7/365.

Let me suggest one more option for a permanent building or facility: an existing church building. As you look around your community, you might be surprised to find an available church building. Sadly, as more and more churches are dying, their facilities are going up for sale. You might be able to lease or purchase an existing church building, which may limit the modifications you have to make.

You might also be surprised to find an active church that is willing to rent their building. Ideally, perhaps, your services will be held on Sunday mornings. But some new churches meet at different times during the week in order to have a place to meet. I also know of two churches that meet simultaneously on Sunday mornings in the same building. That's rare, but it can work.

Finally, there is one other building you might consider: your current church building! If the demographic you're pursuing in your church plant is different enough from your current church, the potential for confusion is low, and it may allow both churches to use the facility more efficiently. It's a newer concept, which we'll address later, but start thinking of creative solutions.

To recap, here are the building/facility options:

- rent a temporary, Sunday-only location
- rent a Sunday-only location with an additional space for midweek meetings
- rent a permanent location
- purchase a permanent location
- meet in another church's facility
- meet in your own (sending) church facility

When determining the type of building you will need for your new church site, context matters. Before the launch of the church I now pastor, I met with a lot of the pastors in my city. Spring Hill has seen enormous growth over the past ten years—it's one of the fastest growing cities in the United States. For that reason, many new church plants were coming to town. As I spoke with one pastor about the city's growth, I remarked, "If I can't plant a church here, I can't plant a church anywhere." My thinking was that there were enough people to go around.

The pastor immediately replied, "If you think like that, you will fail."

Taken aback by his response, I asked, "What do you mean?"

"Our city is a church-plant graveyard," he said. "Over the past ten years, most of the new church sites that have popped up have failed. The community is tired of new churches. This area may be one of the hardest places to start a new church."

That one conversation completely changed our plans for where our church would meet. Contextually, there was no buzz in the city about a church starting up in a school or a movie theater. That had been done before, and people had watched those churches fail. I decided to find a permanent location right from the get-go. I wanted the community to see stability from the very start. It was the right decision, but it came at a cost: delayed staff hiring and delayed new ministries.

Parking and Visibility

In my years of church planting, I've found some unique locations. The square footage was right. The location was right. The price was right. But then I looked at the parking lot. Some of the most impressive options for a church building have almost no parking available. I've seen new church sites overlook the parking, thinking they can find a solution, such as running a shuttle from offsite parking lots. It usually doesn't work. You're better off making sure upfront there is enough parking to match the number of people your building can hold. If the building can hold 150 adults and kids at one time, make sure you have at least seventy-five parking spots. If your community is heavily made up of families, you might be able to get away with sixty parking spots. But do the math. Don't be blind to the reality that people need easy access to the building from where they park.

They also need to be able to see the building easily. With GPS apps available on everyone's phones, visibility of the physical location is not as vital as it used to be. But it's still important. The best-case scenario is that your building can be seen from the road—ideally a road with plenty of drivers.

Three Big Decisions

What will your church site look like? You may not have all the answers, but these three decisions should be made as early as possible:

1. What path will you take: adopt, foster, plant, or multi-site?
2. What will define the DNA of the new church site?
3. Where will you meet?

Don't rush these decisions. Commit them to prayer. Seek counsel from others who have walked this journey before you. Let the Holy Spirit lead. Find the direction God is leading, and then get the process started.

3

Do You Have Vision?

My church seemed lost.

Specifically, the people in the church seemed lost. I could tell people were falling into patterns and habits. Sunday mornings were on autopilot. Meetings were repetitive. The energy in the church began to decline. After a few years, our new church felt like an old church.

But I couldn't figure out why. I felt as if I was doing everything necessary to lead a successful church. We had vision and mission statements. The primary leadership positions were filled. We had the key ministries a church needs. We were seeking excellence in our activities and ministries. We were sharing the gospel and seeing a few baptisms.

But the church seemed lost. I could sense it.

In my heart, I knew where God was leading us. From day one, the vision he had put in my mind, heart, and soul was still strong.

As I sat in my office one Wednesday afternoon, I prayed for answers. Then it hit me. *I* knew where God was leading our church, but did the people know?

I started by surveying the church staff. One by one, I asked them the same question: "Where is this church going?"

Some staff members quoted our vision statement at the time: "We will make Christ the hub of every home." I then followed up with another question: "What does that look like?" Nobody had a concrete answer.

Other staff members referred to our mission statement: "We will belong, thrive, and go." Again, I asked, "What does that look like?" Again, nobody could tell me.

Next, I asked our elder team the same question: "Where is this church going?" This time, I got more general Bible answers than specific local church answers.

"We are going to make disciples," one replied.

Another elder responded with words similar to Acts 1:8: "We will tell people about Christ in our community, country, and the world."

"What does that look like?" I asked.

No one knew.

Then I started asking key volunteer leaders in our church the same question: "Where is this church going?"

One person replied, "What do you mean?"

"I don't know," the next person said.

I was about to give up hope.

Our church clearly had a problem: No one knew where God was leading us. We didn't have just a problem; we had a *big* problem.

As a church, we were lost at sea.

Worse yet, I had no idea how to fix it. On paper, I could check all the boxes. I felt I was doing all the right things. But I still couldn't answer the question, "Where is this church going?"

Or maybe the answer was *nowhere*.

Sitting in my office on another midweek afternoon, I felt my frustration rising.

"God, if no one knows where you're leading this church, what's the point? Why does this church even exist?"

At that very moment, something clicked. I knew that was the question God wanted me to ask. It was the question that moved the conversation from my head to my heart. God didn't care about checkboxes on a piece of paper. He wanted my heart. He cared about my heart as a leader. And I realized that my heart needed to care more deeply about the people in the church and the community.

I stared out my office window. One of the busiest roads in our city goes right past our church building. The road itself is just far enough away that you can see the silhouettes of people, but you can't see their faces. With my heart open to God's revelation and wisdom, I watched every single car pass. I watched silhouette after silhouette pass by. I began to think about those people. In a city of 50,000, there was a good chance my path would not naturally intersect with many of those people's paths. As I continued to pray, my heart became burdened for their souls. My heart became burdened for their eternity, for their relationship with the God of the universe.

Then God brought Matthew 9:36-38 to mind.

When he saw the crowds, he had compassion on them because they were confused and helpless, like sheep without a shepherd. He said to his disciples, "The harvest is great, but the workers are few. So pray to the Lord who is in charge of the harvest; ask him to send more workers into his fields."

I started wondering how many of those silhouettes were confused and helpless. How many people passing within a hundred feet of our church building were like sheep without a shepherd? How many were living without the hope of Jesus?

At that very moment, the answer to the question, "Why does this church exist?" came rushing into my mind.

We exist because everyone needs the hope of Jesus.

That flash of insight birthed a new vision for our church. More importantly, it ignited a fire in my heart for the lost. I couldn't rest anymore. I wanted every one of those silhouettes to know the hope of Jesus like I do.

As soon as I could, I called an elder meeting. While the elders were finding their places at the table. I tacked a big white sheet of paper on the wall.

"Do you remember the question I asked each of you a while back?" I began. "'Why does this church exist?' Well, I have a story for you." Then I shared what God had been doing in my heart. At the end, I wrote in big, bold letters on the sheet of paper, "We exist because everyone needs the hope of Jesus."

Then I turned to the group and asked, "Where are we going now?"

The following year proved to be pivotal for our church. While the world around us seemed to crumble, we remained steadfast in our calling and vision. Without that vision, I don't know where we would be today.

A Vision That Inspires Action

A new church site must have a vision that inspires action.

Many people more knowledgeable than I have written about what makes a great vision statement. I encourage you to find some of those resources and follow what they advise.

As you develop your vision statement for your new church site, be sure to answer the following two questions:

1. Does your vision inspire action?
2. Does your vision communicate why your church exists?

In my current church, we are on our third vision statement in five years. Not because we keep changing our minds, but because we realized that our first two attempts failed to motivate our people to action.

Our initial vision, in its simplest form, read, "Belong. Thrive. Go." We reminded our people every week to "belong to the body of Christ, thrive in community, and go in service." But though that vision statement told people *what* to do, it failed to motivate them.

Our second vision statement was "Making Christ the hub of every home." This vision captured the hearts of our people. They loved the idea that Jesus would be the center of every home in our community. But we discovered a problem: No one knew *how* to make Christ the hub of every home. The vision inspired people, but it didn't lead to action.

When we finally answered the question, "Why do we exist as a church?" it changed our direction. Our vision statement now reads, "We exist because everyone needs the hope of Jesus." This statement clearly communicates why we exist. At the same time, it tells our people what we are supposed to do. If everyone needs the hope of Jesus, then it's our job to take the hope of Jesus to everyone.

We filter everything we do as a church through this vision. Our kids ministry volunteers do what they do because every child needs the hope of Jesus. In our student ministries, we remind our leaders that every student needs the hope of Jesus. Every week, we remind our hospitality team that every person who walks through our doors needs the hope of Jesus.

As you develop the vision statement for your new church site, I highly encourage you to start with three key words: "We exist to . . ."

I'll add one more element to your vision-casting: *communicate your vision ad nauseam.* I've learned that you can never reinforce your vision enough. I communicate our vision through my sermons. I include it in almost every written communication. At every leader's meeting, I reinforce our vision. The people in your church need to be reminded every week why they are doing what they're doing.

A Mission That Motivates

A vision statement describes what the future looks like. As a church, we do what we do today because of a vision for tomorrow. A mission statement outlines our approach to accomplishing our vision. The vision statement is . . . well, visionary. It inspires people to action. A mission statement is more practical, describing the process or path that people in the church can take to join in what the church is doing.

Most churches have a mission statement—typically three to four words that describe their assimilation or discipleship process. There is a clear direction and a clear call to action. After my church adopted our current vision statement, we looked at the vision statement we were replacing and realized we could turn it into a mission statement.

Our mission statement now reads, "Belong to the body of Christ, give generously, thrive in community, and love others." We often shorten our mission statement to four keywords: "Belong. Give. Thrive. Love." Out of our mission, we created what we call a *church pathway*, which outlines the steps we need to take to accomplish our vision.

THE CHURCH AT SPRING HILL
PATHWAY

BECAUSE EVERYONE NEEDS THE HOPE OF JESUS

Every first-time guest receives a copy of this pathway. From the very beginning, we want every person in our church to be motivated to journey with us in pursuit of our vision.

Find a mission that will motivate your new church congregation. Define the expectations of what it means to be involved in the church. When you have a vision that inspires, it's natural to have a mission that motivates.

A Strategy That Executes

Without execution, vision and mission are empty statements—wishful thinking. Your vision and mission are only words on a page if you don't *do* something with them. Execution is king.

Once people are onboard with the vision and mission, the next logical question is, "How do we accomplish this?" As church leaders and committed church members, we must clearly communicate the strategy so that the vision and mission can be accomplished.

An executable strategy will clearly define the actions needed to accomplish the vision and mission. Whereas your vision and mission are perpetual, strategies are time-oriented. They will change as you go along. If the vision is to climb a mountain, and the mission is the path you will climb, the strategy will define steps needed to get to the next mile marker.

In any twelve-month period, a new church will have anywhere from two to six clearly defined strategies. Using the vision and mission from my current church, let me give you an example of what a yearlong strategy may look like.

If the vision is to share the hope of Jesus, then the strategy to accomplish that vision is to equip and send people into the community. For the entire first year, the church could focus on what it means to *go*. Here's how you might break the year up into five smaller strategies that build on each other:

- Go and Serve (February): Recruit and assimilate new volunteers
- Go and Invite (March and April): Equip and send people to invite others to the Easter service
- Go and Pray (May, June, and July): Equip and send people to prayer walk in the community

DO YOU HAVE VISION?

- Go and Learn (August): Teach people how to share the gospel
- Go and Love (October and November): Send people out to share the gospel in the community

With a clearly defined strategy, church members will know where the church is going and how you're going to get there. There's no wondering what's next. The planning is done; it's time to execute the strategy.

Let me give you a quick warning: If leadership doesn't lay out a clear strategy, two things will happen. Either the vision and mission will fail, or people will begin to create their own strategies. I fear the second one more than the first. If people in the new church start to create their own strategies for accomplishing the vision and mission, the new church site will quickly develop a culture problem. And a lousy culture can soon dismantle a new church site.

A Culture That Bonds

There's a well-known saying in the business world that "culture eats strategy for breakfast."

In other words, you can create a great strategy, but if it doesn't align with the culture of your church, you'll just be spinning your wheels. Your strategies must not only support and enhance your vision and mission, but they must also fit the culture of your organization.

Culture can often be the most challenging part of organizational leadership because it's the least tangible. But culture can be seen in two main ways: by what you *communicate* and what you *celebrate*. These serve to define the *values* of the organization—the things people think are important.

Here's a sample list of values that can create a *bonding* culture:

WE'RE ON MISSION. We are people who live our lives in ways that point to the hope of Jesus.

WE PRIORITIZE PRAYER. We are people who depend entirely on God. We know that prayer is a posture of the heart, not just an activity.

WE STRIVE TO BE END-OF-THE-LINE LEADERS. Putting others before ourselves helps God's Kingdom advance further.

WE TAKE ACTION. We are committed to our vision and mission, and we will follow through on our commitments.

WE STRIVE FOR EXCELLENCE. It's not about being the best; it's about always doing our best for Jesus.

WE STRIVE TO MAKE CHRIST THE HUB OF OUR HOMES. Our living rooms are our first mission field. We will commit to keeping Christ at the center of our families.

WE'RE ALL IN THIS TOGETHER. We will be a collaborative people—listening to others, living openhandedly, and demonstrating grace.

WE HAVE FUN AND LAUGH OFTEN. Telling other people about the hope of Jesus is fun. We'll be people who take the gospel seriously without taking ourselves too seriously.

WE WILL DO WHATEVER IT TAKES TO ADVANCE THE GOSPEL.
The hope of Jesus is a big message to a big world. We'll do whatever it takes to see that message taken to a world that desperately needs the hope of Jesus.

Communicating the culture of your church is the first step. But culture is also defined by what we celebrate. To use another well-known leadership statement, "What gets celebrated gets replicated." Find ways to celebrate the values of your new church site. Let leaders know when they successfully reinforce the culture. Give small gifts (e.g., church logo stickers or pins) whenever a leader or volunteer lives out the culture. A new church with a healthy bonding culture will carry out strategies to effectively achieve the vision and mission of the church.

A Site Name That Communicates

Whenever I work with church leaders who start a new church site, the name of the church is often the very first decision they make. After the church has a name, they start working on the vision, mission, and culture. Though that approach isn't necessarily wrong, I encourage you to reverse the order. Start with the vision. Work your way down through the mission, strategy, and culture. Once those pieces are in place, the process of naming the new church will happen naturally.

Regardless of the process, make sure the name communicates the vision and mission of the church. Or, at the very least, make sure the name doesn't conflict with the vision and mission. For example, the church I pastor is called The Church at Spring Hill. The name isn't hypercreative by any means. But at its core, it shows that we identify with—and are committed to—the community of Spring Hill. Why? Because we want everyone in our community to know the hope of Jesus. We also could have named the church Hope Church and been consistent with our vision.

In founding a new church site, you may want to retain an identity with the sending church. If that's the case, I suggest finding a balance between the established identity and connecting with the community of the new church site. An easy solution is to take the name of the sending church and add the new community's location. For example, if Grove Church is the sending church and the new church site is located in a town called Hartsville, simply call the new church site Grove Church at Hartsville.

Church Branding

I understand that "church branding" may feel more like a corporation than a church, but it's really just a shorthand way of saying website, logo, font, and colors. Whenever you start a new church site, you must establish the brand so that people start to identify the church in the community. I am not an expert in this field, but I suggest you get some counsel on how best to establish the new church's brand.

Once you've settled on a name that communicates your vision and mission, secure an online domain for your website. Don't wait on this. If possible, use a .com domain. Other commonly used web domains for churches include .church, .org, and .tv.

Create a modern and straightforward church logo. Have the logo professionally designed with multiple applications. There are plenty of online sites that can help you with logo design, including font and colors.[1]

Be Bold

When it comes to your vision, mission, strategy, and culture, be bold. Be bold for Christ. The culture around our churches is changing rapidly. The culture within our churches must be bold for the truth.

The harvest is plentiful, and the workers may yet be few, but it doesn't have to stay that way. Through Christ, develop a vision that inspires people to action. Anchor the actions of the church in that bold vision. Develop a mission that motivates. Develop a strategy that executes. Develop a culture that bonds.

4

Who Will Be on the Team?

STARTING A NEW CHURCH SITE must be a team effort.

Teams can take many shapes and forms, but I would caution against starting a new church site as a lone wolf. I've seen some very high-capacity individuals set out to start a new church site independently. Though the churches often seem to work at first, one of two outcomes usually occurs. Either the church leader gets burned out and the church loses steam, or the church simply stops growing. Successful church planting and growth depend on a vital principle: *delegation*. Also known as sharing the load. Without delegation, your new church site will hit a growth ceiling. This means you're going to need a team.

Let's answer the big question first: Who will be on the team?

Whom Do You Hire First?

When starting a new church site, the ability to hire full-time staff members is a huge blessing; but it doesn't always work that way.

There are many different ways to "hire" the people you'll need—which we'll cover later. For now, let's focus on the roles you'll need to fill.

On-Site Leader

Site pastor, campus pastor, or lead pastor. Whatever title you choose, the on-site leader of the new church site must be the first person you hire. The exact title will depend in part on the site structure—adoption, fostering, planting, or multi-site.

The site structure determines the team structure, which determines the role of the new site leader. But no matter what, the on-site leader must be the first person on the team. Then it's time to build a team, starting with the worship leader.

Worship Leader

On Sunday mornings, the worship leader will have as much visibility as the site pastor. Depending on how you structure the service, the worship leader may be onstage as much as 60 percent of the time. The general perception among the congregation is that whoever is onstage is leading the church. Filling this role early on is critical, but don't rush the decision. The person you choose must be the right fit.

Here are three characteristics I would look for in a worship leader:

1. *Alignment.* The worship leader must align theologically, philosophically, and pragmatically with the vision of the church.
2. *Quality.* There are many well-intentioned but under-equipped worship leaders out there. Don't sacrifice quality just to fill the role.

3. *Consistency and versatility.* Most golfers have at least one club in their bag that they can hit well with almost every time. Likewise, a worship leader may have a favorite song or two. But can he or she adapt and maintain consistency as the music portfolio grows?

Don't be afraid to take a chance on someone with potential. I hit a home run with our current worship leader. He had proven himself as a student worship leader, but before he joined our team, he hadn't led regular worship for adults. Our church was small and young. He brought some much-needed energy and passion to the team and to the church. Each year, he grew as a worship leader and eventually worked himself into a full-time position. If you can't find a proven worship leader, don't be afraid to take a chance on someone with the right heart and the right skill set.

Kids Ministry Leader

If you plan to reach families with children, hire a kids ministry leader. Having a dynamic, safe, and biblically based kids ministry is important for almost every church—including new church sites. Finding a talented and responsible kids ministry leader is a must. In fact, in my current church, the kids ministry leader was the first hire I made. Because our community is full of young families, I knew that a successful kids ministry would be important right out of the gate.

Other Leaders

If you can hire a good on-site leader, worship leader, and kids ministry leader, you'll have the major pieces in place. A case could be made for other ministry positions, as well, but don't fall into the trap of over-hiring at the beginning. There are always exceptions, but for the most part, other staff positions can easily be filled by volunteers. I'm thinking specifically of administrative assistant, facilities, welcome/hospitality team, finance, prayer, and missions.

Hire the Right People

You never really know someone until you have to live or work with him or her.

No one intentionally hires the wrong person. But it can be challenging to discern how someone will fit with your team. Unfortunately, you often won't know whether you've hired the right people until you start working with them—and by then they're already hired!

There are entire books dedicated to hiring the right team members, but let me give you two guidelines that I've found helpful over the years. These aren't new; but you might say they're tried and true.

The Three (or Four) C's

Perhaps you've heard some version of the three C's of leadership. *Character* usually heads the list—for good reason—while the other two C's might include some combination of *chemistry, competence, commitment, communication,* or *capacity.*[1] I've settled on four that may be helpful in evaluating people for your new church site team.

1. *Character.* Does the person live a life of integrity? Does he or she demonstrate a desire for what is right?
2. *Chemistry.* How does the potential team member connect with the existing team?
3. *Competence.* Does the potential team member possess the needed traits and abilities to accomplish the role?

4. *Capacity*. Does the potential hire have the ability to grow and a desire to learn?

Hiring for Weaknesses

There is no perfect staff member. Everybody has strengths and weaknesses. As your team grows, these attributes will overlap and complement one another. But at the beginning of the team-building process, you'll want to try to balance strengths and weaknesses. A simple personality assessment can help you identify key traits. When adding someone to a small team, try to hire a person with strengths that will offset the weaknesses of other team members.

There's Power in Not Hiring Full-Time

The word *hire* often connotes a full-time role. But when starting a new church site, you may have only one or maybe even no full-time team members. Of the four site paths we discussed in chapter two—adoption, fostering, planting, and multi-site—the church planting path is the one most likely to need a full-time person heading it up from the start, but not always. In fact, there's power in not hiring full-time.

The Power of Part-Time

Most church ministry roles do not require forty hours per week. This means full-time staff members are often filling more than one ministry role. Consequently, a full-time staff member must possess the skills needed to lead multiple ministries. Finding a person with the required skills can take a long time and cost the church more money. On the other hand, a part-time staff member can be highly focused and specialized in the specific role they are hired to fill. Because part-time staff members can focus on a single area of ministry, they are usually more effective and efficient in their roles. Choosing to hire part-time instead of full-time can save the church money and time.

Part-time staff members are also an excellent pool for finding higher potential full-time staff. Hiring people part-time allows you to get to know them before you bring them on full-time.

The Power of Contract Workers

Contract workers are similar to part-time staff, with one major difference. Contract workers are hired for a particular project or a specific length of time. Contract workers can also be remote. After the first two years in my current church, we needed to fill an administration and communication role. There was no one in the church who met the four C's, so I hired a remote contract worker. Even though she lived four hours away, she was a vital part of the team. This arrangement worked well for several years.

You can also contract out ministry positions. Setting up a twelve-month contract for a kids ministry leader or worship leader can be a great fit. Having clearly defined expectations and a clearly defined contract length can spare a lot of heartache down the road. It gives the new church site leader a chance to work with a person before making an open-ended commitment in either a part-time or full-time capacity.

The Power of Paid Volunteers

There's a bit of a dance that takes place with the idea of paying volunteers. The term *paid volunteer* is an oxymoron.[2] When you pay a volunteer (say, twenty-five dollars per week) to carry out a role, you gain the significant benefit of accountability. Paid volunteers typically focus on executing a single role. A great example of a paid volunteer position in a young church is the hospitality team (First

Impressions) leader. This doesn't need to be a staff position, but the importance of the role requires accountability.

One quick warning: Some paid volunteers will see themselves as staff members. This shift in perspective may not manifest itself at the beginning, but it may crop up down the road. Therein lies the dance—making sure that *volunteer* is emphasized more than *paid*. Clarity is essential with paid volunteers. If you can find the right paid volunteers, it can benefit the church greatly.

When you utilize the power of paid volunteers, you create a natural hiring pipeline within the church. Here's how this pipeline functions:

Paid Volunteer	→	Contract Worker	→	Part-Time Staff	→	Full-Time Staff

Allow me to illustrate this process with the example mentioned above: the hospitality team leader.

Let's say you decide to pay a volunteer to lead your hospitality team. Let's call her Allison. After a few months of observing Allison's work as an unpaid volunteer, you decide to put her in charge. By agreeing to pay her a stipend for the added responsibility, you gain Allison's buy-in and establish accountability to the pastor or a staff member.

As she continues to excel in her role, it becomes evident that she has made many connections in the congregation and the church is naturally growing. Soon you realize that you need someone to help assimilate the new people into the life of the church. You approach Allison with an offer to become a one-year contract worker to oversee both the hospitality team and the assimilation team.

Allison is now fully invested and active in carrying out the vision, mission, strategy, and culture of the church. It's obvious she is passionate about people and seeing them come to know (and grown in) Jesus.

Over the next few months, you determine that Allison should be more than a one-year contract worker. She has the skills and attributes to lead these two ministries moving forward. So next, you promote her to a part-time staff position. She now casts vision for her two ministries in a way that someone coming in from outside the church never could. She knows the people, she knows the heartbeat of the church's culture, and she knows her role. Though you don't know whether you will expand Allison's role to full-time down the road, you've developed a far more effective part-time staff than if you had hired someone from the outside.

Though it may not always work out to expand someone's role to full-time, or even part-time, using the pipeline approach gives you a natural process for finding qualified people when more leadership is needed in the church. And it gives people an opportunity to demonstrate their abilities in ways you couldn't otherwise see.

There's power in using paid volunteers. They just might end up as your next full-time staff members.

Paying Your Team

Every new church site leader wants to be autonomous. That's human nature. But it usually doesn't work out that way at first, especially financially. In the next chapter, we'll talk about church finances. For now, here are two ways to pay your team when the church budget doesn't allow for it.

Raising Support

The easiest way to pay team members is to ask them to pay for themselves. In church planting, staff members can be hired with the expectation of raising their own support. This is a time-honored practice in many Christian ministries. However, this approach may make it easy for the church but not for the team members. Still, raising support is one way to bring on new team members without creating a large financial burden for the church.

Having raised support as a church planter, I can offer a few guidelines:

1. The church should pay at least part of the team member's salary. It's unhealthy for a church not to invest in the new venture.
2. The church should have a scaled plan to pay for salaries. The church could start by paying 25 percent, with a plan to increase by 25 percent each year until it reaches 100 percent.
3. Raising support often begins before a staff member joins the team, and raising support is an ongoing process, so it becomes part of the staff member's job. Time for raising support should be included as part of the team member's weekly hours. At least 20 percent of a staff member's hours should be allocated to raising support.

A Single Donor

Though it's rare, another way to underwrite team member salaries is to find a donor, or donors, to put up a stipend. It takes a wealthy individual to be able to pay for a part-time or full-time salary. But there may be people in your congregation who can do that.

As with raising support, this method needs a few guidelines:

1. Set a time frame. I recommend no longer than three years. There is risk involved when a single donor is paying a salary.

2. Let the staff member know the financial situation and set the expectation that he or she will help the church grow to where it can financially pay team member salaries.

3. Set the expectation with the new site congregation that the church will pay the staff members' salaries as the church grows.

A Commitment to Excellence

Every team member must demonstrate a commitment to excellence. New church sites are fragile ecosystems. Every team member must be willing to play their respective roles to the highest standards. They must care about the details. They must not cut corners. They must strive to get things right the first time and look for ways to do things better the next time. If a commitment to excellence is not part of the new church site's team culture, it will create a culture of apathy in the church. If the leaders don't care, you can't expect others to care.

At my church, we have a catchphrase: "Strive for excellence. It's not about *being* the best; it's about always *doing our best* for Jesus." Set the tone for excellence early at your new church site. Provide accountability for the things that matter. Lovingly push your team to carry out their roles with efficiency and effectiveness. Reward your team when they go above and beyond expectations. In your role as a leader, demonstrate what it looks like to do all things with excellence.

We can always do our best for Jesus.

5

How Much Is This
Going to Cost?

You will either love this chapter or want to skip it altogether. I've found there is little middle ground when it comes to the financial aspects of starting a new church site. Creating a budget, raising funds, and handling money motivates some leaders; others want to run away from it all and keep their focus on other parts of ministry. But no matter which side you fall on, finances are vital for starting a new church site.

The financial picture will vary, depending on which path you choose. A church plant may be more heavily focused on raising funds, whereas a multi-site campus launched by an existing church may have more financial backing from the start. But every new church site must have a solid financial plan—otherwise, your success will be limited.

Creating a Budget

Two budgets are needed for a new church site: a *start-up* budget and an *ongoing* budget. The start-up budget will include several one-time costs that will not be a part of the ongoing church budget.

Start-up Budget

The best way to determine your start-up costs is to plan out your first service. Think through every detail of what you will need to start. How do you envision the worship service? When people walk through the doors for the first time, what will they experience? What will your kids ministry look like? For every part of your first service, make a list of all the supplies you'll need. I know the process can be tedious, but it's better to have an idea of what it will take to launch than to neglect a key element. Though each new church site will have different needs, here are some general categories of start-up costs:

- *Branding:* What will it cost to create a logo, color palette, website, and promotional materials (e.g., T-shirts, hats)?
- *Worship supplies:* Do you need speakers, a soundboard, chairs? What about a video projection system? And don't forget about lighting.
- *Kids ministry supplies:* Teaching materials, toys, craft supplies, and changing tables are just the beginning.
- *Setup and teardown:* If you are meeting in a temporary space, you will need a plan to set up and tear down each week. Can you store your supplies on-site? If not, you'll need to prepare for a trailer and storage space.
- *First impressions/hospitality:* Do you plan to give first-time guests a gift? What about a welcome center?

Yearly Budget

Your first-year budget will be a bit of a guess. It's hard to know what you will spend and how much you will receive in financial support. You can start in one of two ways: (1) create a budget based on estimated giving, or (2) create a budget based on known costs (e.g., rentals, salaries, supplies, equipment). If you have a launch team, ask them to commit to an annual giving amount. This might seem intrusive, but knowing that will help you budget and be a better steward. And people tend to rally around what they have an investment in.

Whichever approach you take, I suggest you create a three-year budget plan. Plan for increased costs and increased giving from year to year. New church sites typically see substantial percentage increases in both costs and giving over the first three years. For example, my current church saw a 41 percent giving increase from year two to year four. But our costs went up significantly as well. Put together a plan that demonstrates growth.

Here are some noteworthy "budget buckets" to consider for a yearly budget:

- facilities
- salaries
- ministries
    - administration
    - worship
    - students
    - kids
    - discipleship
- missions

Finding Financial Partners

If you wanted to skip this chapter, this might be the section you'll want to read the least! Very few people enjoy raising money. I've done it for three church plants now, and it hasn't gotten any easier. However, I learned some tips along the way. Here are a few of them.

Develop a prospectus. Whenever you schedule a meeting to ask potential donors for a financial gift, don't show up empty-handed. Even more, don't show up with a poorly produced presentation. Take the time to create a professionally designed prospectus. Combine your vision, mission, strategy, budget, community demographics, and a few powerful testimonials into a single document that you can give to potential donors. More than likely, you will not receive a financial commitment on the spot. Leave them with something they can review and pray over after the meeting.

Make the ask! After years of raising funds for church plants, I've learned that the most important part of raising money is asking for the funds. Sometimes I've started conversations with upfront honesty: "I'm asking you for money." It sets the expectation at the outset. Now, that's not always the best approach. You have to know your audience before making an upfront request like that. But no matter where it comes in your presentation, don't beat around the bush. Ask for the contribution.

Individuals and organizations. Seek out both individuals and organizations. Typically, individuals like to give ongoing gifts (such as a monthly amount), while organizations may prefer to make a one-time contribution. The best time to ask organizations for financial support is late summer. Churches often do their budget planning in the early fall if their fiscal year aligns with the calendar year. Ask for a contribution from their next budget year or a gift out of this year's surplus (if they have one). If you wait until January or February to ask, you've missed a key window of opportunity.

Follow up. If you don't get a commitment during the meeting, then following up is a must. Immediately after the meeting, write a handwritten thank you note and get it in the mail. Yes, you could send an email, but a handwritten note is far more personal and effective. A week or two later, follow up with an email or a phone call. Make sure your potential financial partner has an opportunity to ask more questions and knows the best way to get the money to you. Be gently persistent without being annoying.

Creating a Foundation Board

With my third new church, I created a foundation board to take responsibility for raising 75 percent of the needed funds. After our first year at the new site, we were able to dissolve the board because we had sufficient funding. This concept may not work in every situation, but it worked for us, and I believe it is worth consideration.

The foundation board had five members, and they were tasked with three responsibilities:

1. Raise 75 percent of the needed funds.
2. Oversee the handling of the new church's finances through the end of the first year.
3. Provide financial accountability during the start-up.

I was able to cast enough vision to the five members in a way that they wanted to share it with others—despite the fact that I wasn't very good at vision-casting at the time. These foundation board members not only saw the spiritual need, but they also saw the solution and understood what it would take to make it happen.

They believed in the vision of the church because they saw my heart for the community.

As the vision spread, so did the network of potential donors. We were no longer dependent on only the people I knew. While I focused on my own network for the other 25 percent of the funds, money came in from a lot of people I didn't know personally. I encourage you to give it a try. The same idea might work for you.

Handling Money

Nothing will create distrust in a new church faster than mishandling money. Right from the get-go, before the new church even launches, you must have solid financial systems in place. Even if you don't utilize a foundation board, make sure you have a financial team with knowledgeable, trustworthy members.

Creating a finance team before the church launches forces the founding leadership to set up systems with accountability and transparency. It also communicates to the congregation that reliable systems are in place—which builds trust.

For the finance team, create checks and balances with adequate oversight. One person should never be solely responsible for receiving, tracking, and distributing the funds. Your finance team should have at least three people: one who receives the funds, one who tracks the funds, and one who distributes the funds. For additional security, you might want to require a second signature on expenditures above a certain level. Every area of financial management should be visible to every person on the team. Do monthly financial reviews and a yearly financial audit.

Create financial transparency with the congregation as well. Provide a weekly report of money received and money spent. At my church, we provide a weekly report of the following:

- month-to-date budget
- month-to-date giving
- previous month's budget
- previous month's giving
- year-to-date budget
- year-to-date giving

In addition to your weekly reporting, make sure the annual budget has buy-in from the congregation. I know this may look different from one church to the next, based on church polity. But in whatever way you can get buy-in, I recommend it.

Vision-Casting and Church Finances

The Bible talks a lot about money. It gives us guidance on how we are to give—joyfully and generously. It provides many reasons for why we give—starting with the fact that everything we have belongs to God. As a pastor, take time to teach your congregation about biblical giving. If the people in your new church site develop a biblically based conviction about giving, it will likely result in bringing in the financial support the church needs to operate well and accomplish the vision.

Along with laying a biblical foundation for giving, start casting a financial vision as well. As much as we might hope that biblical conviction alone will motivate people to give, it never hurts to paint a compelling picture of why they should give to the local church. People like to know that the money they give is used for a good purpose.

Here are two ways to cast a vision that will propel giving in your new church site:

1. *"Because you gave, this happened."* Tell stories on a regular basis about the direct effect of the church's generosity.

Testimonials are powerful motivators. One of the best connections you can make is between the ministries of the church and baptisms or changed lives. As the church's ministries begin to have an impact in the community, "good news stories" can become a regular part of your church services.

2. *"When you give, this will happen."* Clearly communicating the church's vision, mission, and strategy will create a lot of forward-thinking in your congregation. Remind people that when they give, they are supporting these future ideas. Provide specific examples of how financial gifts will be used to advance the church's strategy. Remind people that their giving enables the church to be a blessing in the community.

Keeping the Faith

Raising financial support for a new church site can be a difficult process. You'll hear *no* a lot of the time—or "let me think about it." And though you want people to pray about their giving, you'll find that some will use "let me pray about it" as a dodge as well. At times it may feel as if you're continuing to ask and no one is responding. But then you'll get that *yes*. You'll get that positive response that encourages you to keep moving forward. You'll be reminded that God has the whole thing in his hands.

Learning how to trust God to provide financially for your new church site will build your faith. When we started the church I now pastor, we needed $75,000 for start-up costs. I thought there was no way we would reach that goal. But I started praying. In November 2014, I asked God for two things: enough families to start one Bible study, and $50,000 to get our plans off the ground.

Within six weeks, four families committed to attend a weekly Bible study, and we raised $47,000.

God showed me that he provides in unimaginable ways. I encourage you to memorize Ephesians 3:20-21 as you begin planning your new church site.

Now all glory to God, who is able, through his mighty power at work within us, to accomplish infinitely more than we might ask or think. Glory to him in the church and in Christ Jesus through all generations forever and ever! Amen.

God works in ways we can't fathom. Have faith. Trust him.

6

What's Under the Hood?

I'M NOT REALLY INTO CARS, but I enjoy watching vintage car auctions every so often. Car enthusiasts love to talk about the history and performance of their cars. They also love talking about the various parts of their vehicles—from body design to engine type to wheel size. There are some parts they never talk about—such as fuel lines, electrical wires, and pumps. But without those parts, the cars wouldn't run. You can have the best engine, fuel mixture, and tires, but if they aren't all connected and working together, the car won't do what it's designed to do.

The same is true of church systems. It's not a frequent topic of conversation, but without good systems in place, the church cannot operate at its full potential. Though it may not be exciting to develop the systems for your new church site, my hope in this chapter is that you'll at least understand their importance. Good systems are important for any church, but they are essential for a new church site. I wouldn't launch a new church without three primary systems in place: *administration, finances,* and *assimilation.*

These systems take time and forethought to develop. Don't rush the process. The advantage of starting a new church site is that you can create your systems from the ground up. But that's also a big responsibility. Some of the decisions you make at the beginning will have long-lasting effects.

Administrative Systems

Your administrative systems are some of the most important ones you will develop. Many of these systems will require input from lawyers, accountants, and established church leaders. Make sure you've done your homework on these before you start your new church site.

Corporate structure. If your new church site is entirely autonomous from an existing church, you will need to establish a corporate structure. In the United States, churches are legal entities. The new church site will need to go through the nonprofit/501(c)(3) decision process. If you are associated with a denomination, your headquarters can be a great resource. It may be possible to incorporate under the denomination's 501(c)(3) umbrella.

State compliance. Just as churches are recognized as legal entities at the federal level, they are also recognized on the state level. Chances are you will need to register your church site with your state authorities as well. This process is usually less cumbersome than establishing the 501(c)(3) corporate structure, but it's still something that needs to be done.

Church bylaws and constitution. There are entire books on the topic of church bylaws and constitutions. I encourage you to utilize some of these resources. But let me give you a few tips I've learned along the way regarding church bylaws.

1. Do your research. Find two or three other churches that operate the way you want your new church to operate. Ask to see their bylaws. With their permission, pull out pieces from each to create your own.
2. Make your bylaws as simple as possible. Create bylaws that give you just enough structure so you can operate. Don't add specific ministry guidelines and policies to the bylaws.
3. Bylaws are guardrails, not strict policies. They are intended to create operational safety in the church, not to set the direction for ministry. Don't establish a precedent early on that the church's bylaws determine the functions of each ministry.

Insurance. Every church needs insurance. Even if you don't own anything, you need liability insurance. Explore whether the new church will also need counseling insurance, lawsuit insurance, and (unfortunately) child abuse insurance.

IRS sales tax exemption. Nonprofits get a great benefit by not paying sales tax on purchases (in states that have sales tax). Every state differs in how they approve and provide this exemption. Also, every business has its methods for handling the sales tax exemption form. It's worth the effort and time to set up the exemption, especially with businesses you buy from frequently.

Financial Systems
In all my years of ministry, I've never had someone walk up to me and say, "I'd like to be the church treasurer." (And if anyone ever did, I probably wouldn't make them the church treasurer.) The most qualified will likely never volunteer for the role. They know what the role entails, and they don't want to jump in.

That said, it's important to find someone to oversee the church's financial operations as soon as you can. But it has to be the right person. I would rather have a volunteer with the right heart and limited experience than someone with loads of experience who cannot be trusted. Ability can be taught; integrity cannot.

Even if you don't have anyone in this role at first, there are some financial systems you'll need to get started.

Banking. Open a bank account as soon as you can. Many banks require the documentation mentioned in the administration section above to open a business banking account. Start building a relationship with a local bank. Ask them what they need from you to open an account.

Digital giving. About 90 percent of my current congregation gives digitally—whether it's by ACH, credit card, text giving, or app giving. Digital giving is easy and convenient. It allows people to set up recurring giving, which is excellent for budget planning. Once your bank account is set up, find an online-giving vendor. They're out there. But even if you don't move into text giving or app giving right away, provide a way for people to give online. I recommend finding a digital-giving vendor who can also supply church management software.

Accounting software/bookkeeping. Once you've opened a bank account, establish your accounting/bookkeeping system. If you wait on this, you're only creating a lot more work for yourself. If you can start using some online accounting software right away, do it.[1] You might want to find a "paid volunteer" bookkeeper. Some church management systems accommodate both digital giving and bookkeeping. From my experience, I would not go that route. I would keep your accounting systems separate from your digital-giving systems. I've found that new church sites will often change their church management systems and their digital-giving systems before they find the best fit. It is a lot more difficult to change your accounting software. When you keep your accounting software separate from other church systems, the entire platform stays nimble.

Assimilation Systems

Administrative and financial systems are obviously important in any organization. One other system that is vital to ministry is an assimilation system—which is designed to help you connect with the people in your church and the people who come into contact with your church.

Church Management Software

Even before you launch your new church site, you'll want to find a way to gather and track people's information. You can start with a simple Excel spreadsheet, but there's value in paying for a system specifically designed for this purpose. You should be able to find a church management software that fits your budget and your needs. I also recommend using an online system that can grow with your church.

We currently use Planning Center Online, but I've used several other systems over the years.[2] Planning Center utilizes an a la carte approach. You can select the modules you want to use. The cost is less for smaller churches.

What should you look for in a church management system? Here's a quick list:

- *Affordability:* Some systems can grow with your church.
- *Ease of use:* Make use of trial periods. If it isn't easy to use, don't get it.
- *Member interaction:* Are church members able to interact with the management software?

- *Digital giving:* Ideally your digital giving system will have some form of app or text giving.
- *Communication:* If you can find a church management system that also has email and text communication features, that's a win/win. If not, look for a stand-alone communication system that has text and email at a minimum.
- *Kids ministry check-in:* You'll need this function sooner than later.

Guest Follow-Up

The easiest way not to grow as a church is by failing to follow up with new families that come in. Plan, process, and execute a guest follow-up system from day one. Here's a simple procedure that you can start right away:

1. Provide information for guests and newcomers on your church website.
2. Create a hospitality/first impressions team for worship services. This team will be responsible for creating a welcoming appearance in the entryways, greeting people, and providing information for guests and newcomers.
3. Give each first-time guest a gift (e.g., a church mug).
4. Ask guests to fill out a connection/communication card.
5. Write a thank-you note to each guest who attends for the first time.
6. Follow up with an email one week later, inviting them back to church.

There's no doubt you can add more steps to my example. But more important than the specific details is making sure you follow through on the process. I've seen fantastic, well-designed guest follow-up systems that never get implemented. And I've seen very simple follow-up systems that produce great results because the church actually follows up. Find what works best for your congregation and follow up with every guest.

Volunteers and Membership

You don't have to do this *before* you launch your new church site, but within the first six months after opening, you'll want to create a system that moves people from *attenders* to *volunteers*. A significant first step is to create a class where people learn how their gifts and talents can be used in the church. Then, within the first twelve months, create a system that moves people from *attenders/volunteers* to *members*. Churches typically use a membership class for this.

Communication Systems

People won't come if they don't know about your new church. And these days, people won't come to your church if they can't find you online. People like to be able to go online and find useful information about the church. In some cases, online information is valued and trusted more than speaking with someone face-to-face about the church. Knowing that your online presence will likely be the first impression many people have of your church, you want to get it right. It doesn't have to be fancy or complicated, but it should be user-friendly. It should be easy to find and navigate, and should give people the information they need to come check you out.

Church Website

There's really no reason not to have a good website. I'm still amazed when I stumble on a church website that looks like it was designed in the 1990s. You don't need a lot of bells and whistles, but your site must look fresh and up to date, and it needs to be *maintained*.

A church's website is the new front door of the church. Many people will decide whether to attend a church based on the website. If you don't have a website at all, there's only a 1.4 percent chance that someone will find and attend your church. I made up that statistic, but it's probably true (and you get the point). Make sure your new church has a good website.

If you don't know where to begin, you can try one of several "build it yourself" websites for a minimal cost.[3] There are also several companies online that specialize in designing church websites.[4] They offer low-cost options with support and help. If you know nothing at all about websites, I recommend going with one of those vendors. You don't need the best website ever, but make sure it's good.

Social Media
You don't need to be on every social media platform right from the beginning. Start with what you can manage. Creating a Facebook page is often a good first step. Customize the page using your logo and information. Update your page once or twice a week with relevant information. Keep it simple. It's better to have good content than an abundance of bad content.

Google Maps
When people look for a church, they will most likely use Google. Among the various search engines, Google is chosen 85 to 90 percent of the time.[5] Depending on how people search for your church, there's a good chance they'll end up on Google Maps. You have to walk through a few steps to get your church onto Google Maps, but take the time to do it.

Email

If you collect only one piece of information from guests and attenders at your new church site, make sure it's their email address. Email is still the primary method of communication for most churches. There's a place for other communication methods (e.g., texting), but email is the core. Start a weekly email within the first six months. Most likely, your new church management software can help you send out churchwide emails.

Remember Your Purpose

I get it. Developing and implementing church systems is not high on the list of exciting parts of starting a new church site. But church systems are needed because they serve a larger purpose. They connect the primary ministries of the church so that the church's overall ministry can run well. A well-created, well-run church system may never be noticed. But a poorly run system will stick out like a sore thumb. Create the necessary church systems, and use them well so there will be fewer distractions and hindrances to sharing the hope of Jesus.

7

Where Are the People?

"Hey, Jess, do you have time to meet?"

As I mentioned before, anytime someone starts with, "Hey, Jess," my heart skips a tiny beat. This time, the conversation wasn't going to be bad, but it also wasn't going to be enjoyable.

There was a family I had been trying to draw into a leadership role. That should have been my first clue: I was trying to *draw* them into leadership. After months of meeting and planning, I noticed a change with them. They started attending worship services less often. When they did attend, they came late and left early. Their communication became less frequent, and when we did talk, there was a distance between us. So when they asked me if I had time to meet, I knew what was coming.

A Lesson Learned with People

The conversation I was about to have with this family was one I'd had many times before. It was "the breakup talk." You know how it goes: "It's not you, it's me." It's that "we feel led to" conversation. I was prepared this time.

As I walked up to their house, they were sitting on the front porch. Their choice of casual seating outdoors was another indication that they wanted the conversation to be short and sweet. We weren't going to have coffee and donuts in their living room.

Before they could say anything, I started the conversation.

"When are you leaving?"

I could tell they were surprised. I don't know whether they were surprised that I knew they were leaving, or that I would start the conversation that way. Maybe they were surprised by both. I could also tell they were relieved. I had broken the ice, so they didn't have to.

The conversation went as well as it could. We talked about what other churches in the area might be "the best fit" for them (a different discussion for another chapter). I appreciated their desire to communicate to me what they were doing. It's much better than when a family just disappears (that's also another conversation for another chapter). With more than a few discussions like this one throughout my church-planting years, I've learned a lesson when it comes to people at new churches: *God brings in specific people at specific times for specific purposes to start a church.*

Knowing this doesn't make it any easier. It's still tough when a family that has been with you from the very beginning tells you they are moving away. Or when a family you walked with in the trenches wants to move on to another church. It always stings a little when someone leaves. Sometimes it stings more than others. But when someone leaves your new church, it never feels good.

But before you get discouraged, there's another side to when people leave: *God will bring in someone new*. He uses specific people to move a new church in the direction he wants. The reason it's painful when people leave is that it might keep us from going in the direction we wanted to go. But instead of seeing that as a bad thing, see it as God's grace and mercy. He might want to move your church in an entirely new direction. To change your compass headings, God may allow someone to leave but then bring in someone new.

This has happened in my church several times. God allowed key people to leave, which kept us from moving in a particular direction. Then he brought in someone new who helped us move exactly where we were supposed to go. The hard part is trusting God with the people in your church. Let me break down the lesson I learned into several key points.

- *God brings in:* You must trust that God will always supply what you need as a church leader.
- *Specific people:* The people you think you want in your church may not be the people you need. Be open to new leaders.
- *At specific times:* Trust God's timing. You might go weeks, months, or even years without the people you need. You might not see the reason until later down the road.
- *For specific purposes:* Just because you have a key family or two that can help you grow the church in a particular direction doesn't mean that's where God wants you to go. If God isn't in it, don't run after it.

I hope that you can learn this lesson early on and apply it. It all starts with your launch team.

Assembling a Launch Team

My wife and I were sitting at our kitchen table. I remember her exact words clearly: "I believe God is calling us to start another church." I had sensed that was the direction God was leading us, but I didn't want to believe it. A third church plant in five years felt overwhelming. Rachel was right (as she usually is), and we began the process of starting a new church in the community where we were living.

When God responded to our prayers by providing start-up funding and a few families to build around, I knew the next challenge would be assembling a launch team.

What's a launch team? Nelson Searcy and Kerrick Thomas give the best definition I've seen:

> A team of committed individuals who will assist you in preparing for and executing an effective launch. This is a team of people currently living in the area where your new church will meet—a team that you will build from scratch. The launch team is in existence only through the first weekly service.[1]

No matter what kind of new church site you're starting, you need a launch team. Let's break down the characteristics of a clearly defined launch team:

Purpose. The launch team has one purpose only: to get the new church site up and running. All the conversations and activities of the launch team should focus on what is needed to get the new church site started. You will be tempted to pull your launch team into conversations about ministerial decisions and church leadership issues.

WHERE ARE THE PEOPLE?

But don't do it. Broadening the scope of the launch team's involvement will only create confusion and make the team less effective.

People. Anyone can be on the launch team. Any skill level can be useful. Any level of spiritual maturity. Just make sure the people are local. They must be physically present to carry out the required functions of the team.

Timing. The launch team disbands when the new church holds its first service. Make the timing abundantly clear at the very beginning. Repeat it often. Because of connections that have been built, it can be tempting for a launch team to want to continue meeting after the church has been launched. Instead, the members of the launch team should be released into the church's various ministries. This will counteract the mindset that "we were here first."

Action driven. Members of the launch team should participate in small groups, where they can experience spiritual growth. The launch team is not designed for spiritual growth. The launch team is built for action.

After the parameters of the launch team have been clearly defined, the natural next question is, "Where do I find the people for it?" If you're launching from an established church, you already have a great pool of people. Just look around on Sunday mornings. There are potential team members who gather with you for worship every week. Start casting vision to your current church to attract a launch team. And don't be afraid to ask for specific time commitments. Some people will be willing to serve on the launch team only, others will commit for a longer stint, and some will move permanently to the new church site. Remember, you aren't "losing" these people. You are equipping them for service and utilizing them for growth!

If you are starting a new church site from scratch, start building relationships in your community. This process will take longer than pulling people from an existing church, but it will also produce a clear focus on engaging with the community. When Rachel and I began forming the launch team for our current church, we started with our neighbors. It made sense to reach those directly around us first. Our launch team started with eleven families from our neighborhood of about one hundred homes.

In the next chapter, we will look at what a launch team does in the months and years leading up to the launch. For now, start planning and praying for the people who will join your launch team.

The second half of Acts 2:47 says, "Each day the Lord added to their fellowship those who were being saved." Every week during our launch team meetings, we had what we called the Acts 2:47 Board, where we wrote the names of people who either needed a relationship with Jesus or who might join the launch team. Start praying for your launch team now.

Letting the Community Know

The goal of every new church is to reach their community with the gospel. So you want to start letting the community know about your new church site as soon as possible. But before you get the word out, you must reach a level of preparedness. Very few people will jump in with a new church if it seems unorganized. And there's a good chance that people who hear about a disorganized new church will never give it a try. Here are three key questions to answer before you announce your plans to the world:

1. **WHEN DOES THE CHURCH LAUNCH?** Answering this question means you have done a lot of the preparation. I will give you a calendar in the next chapter to help you determine your launch date.

2. **WHERE WILL THE CHURCH MEET?** I know the church isn't a building, but almost everyone in your community connects the word *church* with a location. Whether you're meeting in a home, an existing church, a business workplace, a warehouse, a school, or a movie theater, be ready to answer the *where* question. If you're meeting in a nontraditional way or location, be prepared to communicate your vision for your location.

3. **WHAT DOES IT LOOK LIKE TO BE INVOLVED RIGHT NOW?** With a new church site, there are so many possibilities for getting people involved before launch: small groups, launch team, monthly preview services, missions teams, discipleship, and more. I recommend having only a few options. Don't overextend yourself before launch. But do have a clear path for someone in the community to get involved.

Once you have those three key questions answered, you're ready to start getting the word out! It's essential to be strategic in your communication. Are you asking the community to join the launch team? Are you asking them to save the date for the launch? Are you asking them to come to a preview service? Make sure you focus on a single message when you start communicating about the church. Once you have the messaging down, you can get the word out in several ways.

Invitation cards. The best way to get a person involved with your new church site is with a personal invitation. Letting someone see the passion on your face for what God is doing is irreplaceable.

It creates opportunities for people to ask questions. And it provides a personal connection to the church site. Research has shown that 82 percent of unchurched people are open to attending church if someone will invite and accompany them.[2] To help with the personal invitation, print some small cards (business card size or slightly larger) and hand them out to your launch team. Always keep a supply of invitation cards in your pocket or bag. Once the launch date arrives, you can switch to a general invitation card going forward.

Social media ads. Social media is the most widespread and least expensive platform for letting the community know about your new church site. My top two recommendations are Facebook and Google Ads. You can set a budget with defined demographics. Just make sure you have a good website!

Preprinted postcards. For years, sending postcards was the primary method for new church sites to communicate to the community. Postcards have taken a back seat with the rise of technology and social media, but they are not obsolete. Targeting a defined area in your community with postcards is still effective. Also, sending postcards to people moving in to your community is a great way to make contact.

Handwritten notes. This method of communication takes a lot of time and energy, but it is highly effective. We've lost the art of handwritten notes, but they will almost always grab someone's attention. By taking the time to write a message to a targeted area of your community, you are almost guaranteed they will read it. You can find companies online that sell lists of addresses in your community. Get a list and write some handwritten notes.

Typed letter with a hand-addressed envelope. Type a generic letter and sign it at the bottom. Then handwrite the address on the envelope. When a person looks through their mail and sees a

YOU'RE INVITED!
6.12.23

JOIN US SUNDAYS
AT 10:00 AM

MEETING AT
4922 PORT ROYAL RD
SPRING HILL, TN 37174

For more information, visit u
ChurchatSH.c

Launch Team Invite Card, front

YOU'RE
INVITED

THE CHURCH
AT SPRING HILL

Invite Card, back

YOU'RE INVITED!

JOIN US SUNDAYS AT
10:00 AM

MEETING AT
4922 PORT ROYAL RD
SPRING HILL, TN 37174

For more information, visit us at
ChurchatSH.com

General Invite Card, front

handwritten address, they will almost always open the envelope. I actually prefer this approach over postcards and handwritten notes, because it takes less time and energy than handwritten notes and is more effective than postcards. This method of communication is also a great way to get your launch team or partner churches involved. Have them write the addresses, stuff the envelopes, and stamp them for you. In my current church, we enlisted "$44 mission partners." At the time, the cost of a stamp was 44 cents. We sent each partner one hundred signed letters with envelopes and asked them to purchase one hundred stamps. They would then address and stuff the envelopes, add stamps, and drop them in the mail. We sent out thousands of letters this way and saw a great return.

However God leads you to let your community know about your new church, always cover your efforts with prayer. Pray for high impact. Pray for the effectiveness of your communication. Pray for receptive hearts in your community. Pray that God will add people daily to your fellowship.

8

What's the Plan?

You know God has called you to start a new church site. He has given you a clear vision, mission, and strategy for the new church. You've planned who will be on the launch team, and you've started the fundraising process. All your plans seem to be on track.

Now it's time to move from ideas to action.

Over years of watching new churches start, I've noticed a natural leaning among church leaders toward either ideation or execution. Some leaders love to plan and theorize about starting a new church. Other leaders just get out there and start without much thought to what's next. If you're one who loves execution, there's a good chance you opened the book to this chapter first.

Every leader of a new church site must know when to plan and theorize and when to take action. This chapter will help you form a plan you can implement.

Let me pass along some good advice I was given when I first started church planting: *A plan that is 80 percent complete is 100 percent ready.*

If you're cringing and thinking, *There's no way I can start something that hasn't been fully thought through!* let me remind you that there will be plenty of other planning to do along the way to starting a new church site. You don't have time to make sure every plan is absolutely foolproof before you take action. There is very little return on investment for the time spent going from 80 percent ready to 100 percent ready when planning. Almost all plans change as you go along anyway. Better to use your time wisely and effectively than to obsess over the 20 percent.

Or maybe you're thinking, *80 percent? I'll take 50 percent and let's get moving!* Let me caution you: Creating avoidable chaos is not a good strategy when starting a new church site, because launching a new church naturally *generates* chaos. Don't create more by failing to plan. Starting a new church site is fast-paced and requires timely decisions. Mapping out where you're going is essential.

So, what's the plan? It starts with deciding when to launch.

Picking a Launch Date

Even though a year has fifty-two Sundays, you do not have fifty-two options for launching your new church site. You have *three*:

1. *New Year's.* After the Christmas season wraps up, most people's minds go to the new year. They start thinking about new habits they wish to form. People set goals for what they want to accomplish in the next twelve months. Church is often on the list. Starting a new church at the beginning of the year gives you an opportunity to enfold

people at a prime time for action. You may need to allow some time for the holidays to settle, but mid to late January is a great launch time.

2. *Easter.* Most people in the United States still connect Easter to Jesus. Though that cultural norm is fading, Easter may still be a good time to launch. This would be my third choice of the three options because summer is right around the corner. Many churches experience a summer slump, and that can be tough for a new church to weather.

3. *Start of the school year.* For families with school-age children, the beginning of school creates new rhythms and schedules. Picking a launch date to coordinate with the start of the school year can capitalize on these new rhythms. In areas with year-round school, this may not be as good an option—though coming out of summer is still a time when people tend to adjust their rhythms.

So how to pick a launch date? Know your community. Know the context of your new church site. Think about which of those three times of the year people in your community are most likely to attend church. Pick a Sunday in whichever season seems best.

If I had to make a blanket statement, I would choose the beginning of the year as the best launch date. Just be mindful of Super Bowl Sunday and potentially Valentine's Day. Through a series of events that were out of our control, we launched my current church on Sunday evenings for the first three months. The fifth and sixth Sundays after our launch date turned out to be Super Bowl Sunday and Valentine's Day. For those two consecutive Sundays, our attendance was 57 percent lower than our Launch Sunday.

Even with our challenging start, the beginning of the year would still be my top choice for a launch date. Pick a Sunday and start planning. There will be challenges with whatever date you choose. Do your best to stick with the date. Preparing your existing church, assembling your launch team, and connecting with your community are all tied to the launch date.

Preparing Your Existing Church

If you are starting a new church site from an existing church, you need to communicate the *why* long before sharing the *how*. It's easy to want to jump in front of the congregation and share your heart about starting a new church site. God has been working in your heart for months, if not years. You've been praying and planning. But for many people in your church, the idea of launching a new site will be overwhelming and confusing.

Start with the why. Your existing church needs to feel the *need* for a new church site before they ever hear the idea of starting a specific new church site. This process takes time. But doing a good job of establishing the why will make the *how* a whole lot easier.

Start communicating with other leaders and committed members in your church—elders, deacons, directors, staff, and key influencers in the congregation. Focus on your primary leaders. As you share your ideas, you must also be prepared to *listen*. Pay attention to body language. Are they nodding their heads but crossing their arms? Are there more questions than affirmations? More frowns than excitement? If your explanation doesn't seem to be landing right, reevaluate how you're communicating the why. If the vision isn't connecting with your top leaders, take it back to God. Pray. Seek the Holy Spirit's guidance. Hear from God on the next steps before going back to your leaders.

Given the excitement and receptivity of your top leadership, move on to the next layer of key leaders in your church. This group may include key families, small group leaders, and members.

Listen to this group as well. Keep communicating and leading, just as you did for the top leadership. Once one-fourth to one-third of your church feels the need for a new church site, quickly move to the church at large. Depending on your church size and structure, there may be other leaders you must communicate with before communicating with the entire church.

It can be challenging to communicate the *need* for a new church site without saying you are starting a new church site. Telling "stats and stories" is a good approach during this period. Because you have already researched the community for the new church site, start communicating these stats on Sunday mornings. Share your heart for this area and why the people there need Jesus. Spend time meeting new people in this community. Listen to their stories and relate these stories on Sunday mornings. Let your heart be knit with the community before your heart is interwoven with the new church site. When your heart is knit with the community, it's much easier to communicate the need for a gospel presence there.

You have effectively communicated the why when people in your church start asking, "What are we doing to reach that community?" Once it has been established why a gospel presence is needed in the new church site's community, begin to cast a vision for how to reach that community with the gospel. At this point, planting a new church site in that community should make sense. The excitement level in your congregation should be high. And now is the time to start asking for commitments from your existing church. Everyone in your church should agree to support the new venture in at least one of three ways:

- *Prayer commitments:* I hope that every person in your existing church will commit to pray for the new church site and the community. Prayer must be a priority. Without prayer, the new church site won't succeed.
- *Financial commitments:* Ask your congregation to give above and beyond their regular giving. Set a financial goal and ask the church to meet it.
- *Participation commitments:* Find the missionaries in your church—the people who are willing to be sent out. Some people will commit to helping with the new church site for twelve months. Others may help for two years. Some people may join the launch team only. And some may sell their homes and move to the new community to fully participate there.

Starting Small Groups in the Community

Whether you have built a team through an existing church or have gathered people from within your community, start a small group. If you can, start more than one. Make sure that all the small groups are within the defined community of the new church site.

The easiest way to start a small group is by meeting in someone's home. Find a family that lives in the community and ask them to host the small group. Have someone from the launch team or leadership team lead the small group. Whoever will be the site leader should also host and lead a small group.

These initial small groups should have two goals: (1) bringing people in from the community, and (2) multiplying into other small groups. Every small group that starts before the launch date should try to multiply before the launch date. If you start two small groups with people from your launch team, you should have four small groups by the time you launch. Creating the new site's

DNA by growing and multiplying small groups before the launch date will generate greater fruit down the road. It also encourages committed members to step up to increased responsibility as more leadership roles are created. Develop a plan for how you will train and encourage new small group leaders before the church site launches. If you wait until after the launch to figure out small group multiplication, you will limit the growth of your church.

During the first few months at a new church site, new people have few ways to get involved. Creating easy on-ramps into small groups will make the new site "sticky." Entire books have been written about small group ministries. Find a few that will help you develop and implement your model from the very beginning.

Launching Your Launch Team

In the previous chapter, we looked at the purpose of a launch team and how to assemble one. But what does a launch team do? Everyone who has joined the launch team should already believe in the vision and mission for the new site. Your first meeting is about teaching them how to *share* that vision and mission with others. The launch team will be out in the community making contacts and developing relationships. As they do, it should feel very natural to share the vision and mission of the new church site. The vision should feel contagious. Every time you meet with the launch team, keep coming back to, and reinforcing, the vision and mission.

Your second meeting will be about the launch day—which marks the end of the launch team's purpose and participation. Remember, the launch team focuses only on what is needed to get the new site up and running. During this second meeting, work out what needs to happen to prepare for the very first worship service at the new site. By now, the site leader should have thought through most of this already, but the launch team needs to feel a part of the process, and they can help you fine-tune it.

Spend several hours during this second meeting "reverse engineering" the launch. Have the team imagine what the first worship service will look like and work back from there. Here are some questions you should be asking:

- "Where are people going to park? How will they know where to go?"
- "What does the kids ministry look like? How will parents drop off and pick up their kids?"
- What if we need to locate a parent during the worship service?"
- "What does it look like for a guest walking in the door for the first time?"
- "Are we serving coffee and water? Where will it be served and what will the area look like?"
- "Do we need signs to direct people inside and outside the building?"
- "How will the worship center be arranged? Do we need lights, speakers, a projector?"
- "Where will people sit? Are chairs available at the site or do we need to get them?"
- "How do we take up an offering?"
- "How do we know if someone is a first-time guest? Will they fill out a connection card?"
- "Will we have to set up and tear down each week? How will that work?"

These are just a sample of questions your launch team will need to answer in preparation for a successful launch day. Start making lists of all the items that need to be accomplished by then and assign them to members of the launch team. Have people figure out how to achieve their assigned tasks, how long it will take to complete them, and how much it will cost. If there are team members who can oversee a particular ministry area (e.g., hospitality, kids ministry, parking), let them direct other members to get those tasks accomplished. I would avoid calling anyone a "ministry leader" at this point, unless you have already formed a leadership team that will carry on beyond the launch.

After the first two meetings, each subsequent meeting should focus on the vision, mission, and launch day execution. Share stories of relationships built. Celebrate new people who join the launch team. Keep the team focused on their purpose of seeing the new church site up and running.

Demonstrating a Love for Your Community

The best way to launch into your community is by demonstrating a love for your community.

By now, you'll have your launch team formed and maybe a few small groups started. Before you gather for your first worship service, bring everyone together and find ways to demonstrate your love for the community. To do this, you must be *in* the community and *of* the community. And everyone must know that you are there *for* the community. The easiest way to show love for your community is by *getting involved* with the community.

I've found it is far more effective to join in and enhance what is already happening in the community rather than trying to create something new. For example, at one church I helped start, we organized a community field day. We invited families from around the community to come out for a day of games, prizes, refreshments, and a bunch of fun. We brought in an out-of-town student group to host the games and engage with the community. The event flopped. We had more volunteers than we did participants. The community didn't want or need this event, and it showed.

On the other hand, with the same church, we partnered with a local retail center that hosted an annual Easter egg hunt. We provided both financial and volunteer support. The community (and the retail center) loved it. About two thousand people from the community came the first year, and more than three thousand people the second year. We joined in with what the community was already doing, and it was a rousing success.

Find ways to show your love for the community before you launch your new church site. They don't have to be over-the-top events. You can write simple notes of encouragement to healthcare workers. Provide lunch for teachers. Wash cars for free. Provide free water and popcorn at a local event. Encourage your launch team to brainstorm and be creative. Before you launch, find some ways to demonstrate to the community that you love them.

Preview Services

It's much easier to drive a car onto the interstate when you take the on-ramp—though, admittedly, I've never tried any other way, and I don't recommend that you do either. Why is the on-ramp the best way? Because it allows you to build up speed before you get into the chaos of all the traffic. Once you launch your new church site, you'll be moving at full speed. Don't try to go from zero to sixty in one step. Give yourself a ministry on-ramp by offering some preview services.

Preview services are incremental public worship services that lead up to the launch service. Preview services are real worship services that the community can attend. As the term suggests, preview services allow the community to catch an early glimpse of the new church. These services are typically held monthly for three to six months leading up to the launch date. There are many advantages to holding preview services:

- You can learn what works and what doesn't.
- They motivate the launch team to execute their assigned items.
- Preview services build momentum leading up to the launch.
- Many churchgoers want to check out the new church in town. Preview services allow you to filter through the already churched to focus on the unchurched at launch.
- They help grow your launch team.
- They help grow your small groups.
- They allow you to try out different worship leaders if you don't have one yet.
- They give your team something to look forward to.
- They allow your team to invite people from the community.
- They build confidence going into the launch.

One significant advantage of preview services is that people expect mistakes. Preview services allow you to try out new things. If a projector stops working or the lighting flickers, most people won't think twice about it. In fact, if someone has a problem with mistakes during a church service, then a new church probably isn't a good fit for them.

Preview services allow you to identify problems and—more importantly—find solutions. Each preview service will have its own set of problems, so make sure you fix the problems from the previous service so they don't compound. You don't want a pile of problems leading into your launch.

With your launch date in mind, schedule three to six preview services. More than six can cause a loss of momentum, and fewer than three doesn't build enough momentum. Find the number that works best for your launch team and your community. And make sure to invite the community!

A Sample Calendar

How does this all fit together? Below is a thirteen-month calendar with a January launch date. The calendar provides an example of which events will occur each month leading up to Launch Sunday.

January

Determine the site you will start

Develop your vision, mission, strategy, and culture (DNA)

February

Cast the vision to your existing church and begin developing relationships in your community

Develop your leadership team

March

Continue casting the vision to your existing church and developing relationships in your community

Seek prayer, financial, and participation commitments

April

Seek prayer, financial, and participation commitments

Create church systems

May

    Seek prayer, financial, and participation
        commitments
    Assemble launch team
    Secure meeting location

June

    Monthly launch team meeting

July

    Monthly launch team meeting

August

    Monthly launch team meeting
    Community event
    Small groups semester begins (weekly meetings)

September

    Launch team meeting before preview service
    Preview service
    Launch team meeting after preview service
    Small groups weekly meetings

October

    Launch team meeting before preview service
    Preview service
    Launch team meeting after preview service
    Small groups weekly meetings
    Community event

November

Launch team meeting before preview service
Preview service
Launch team meeting after preview service
Small groups semester ends

December

Weekly launch team meetings
Christmas Eve preview service

January

Launch Sunday
Launch team "thank you" party
Small group semester starts
Begin weekly services

The plan is in place.
It's time to launch.
Are you ready?

9

Ready to Launch?

EVERY NEW CHURCH SITE LEADER will be asked the question at some point: "Are you ready to launch?"

The reality of a quickly approaching launch date evokes various emotions. There's excitement and worry. There's confidence and uncertainty. There's laughter and tears. There's calmness and turbulence. But almost every new church leader has one underlying emotion: *doubt*.

As the launch date approaches and the spiritual warfare increases, questions and doubts will be on a playback loop.

- "Are we *really* ready to launch?"
- "What if no one shows up?"
- "Should we push back the launch date a few more months?"

- "What if we didn't plan for the right things?"
- "What if the church fails?"

The questions will be endless and relentless. When doubts arise, here's my advice: Turn it over to God.

Let me show you what that looks like.

- "Are we *really* ready to launch?" No, you're not. You will never be 100 percent ready. But God called you and your team to start this church. Commit the church into God's capable hands.
- "What if no one shows up?" Someone will show up. It might not be as many as you hope, or it may be more than you can imagine. Either way, you can trust that God will draw in the right people at the time. Commit all the people to God.
- "Should we push back the launch date a few more months?" No. There will always be a reason to delay the launch. You will always feel as if you need to do more. But God will provide what you need. Commit your plans to God.
- "What if we didn't plan for the right things?" You won't bat a thousand. But God knows that, and he doesn't want or need you to try to control the church. Give control over to God.
- "What if the church fails?" The church might fail, and that's okay. Remember, it's okay not to succeed. I recently spoke to a church planter who had closed the doors on a church he started sixteen years ago. Though his grief was evident, so was his gratitude for those years of ministry. The church didn't *fail*. The Kingdom impact was

tremendous over those sixteen years. God used the church in mighty ways. Change your definition of failure. And whatever success looks like for you, give it over to God.

The doubts and questions will come, but ultimately it will be time to launch. Faithfully do what God has called you to do and leave the results to him.

Launch

I arrived about four hours early for the launch of my current church. I was the only one in the building. I turned on the lights and the speakers. I filled up the baptistry. I put out the signs. I made sure the bathrooms were clean and the trash cans were empty. Then I sat down in the middle of the worship space.

The past year had led up to this day, to this point in time. I remembered the moment when my wife and I were at the kitchen table and God's calling on our lives became so clear. I remembered the moment when I said *yes* to God to start this new church. That moment of God's calling led to this moment of God's provision. I gave God all the glory. It was time to launch.

Every new church leader wants a successful launch. The first worship service sets the tone for what's to come. What does a successful launch look like? Definitions will vary, but here are some elements you want to make sure you have in place on Launch Sunday:

- *Invite people.* There are very few reasons I would ever postpone the launch of a new church. Not inviting people is one of those reasons. At the bare minimum, the launch team should commit to inviting people. I recommend setting an invitation goal for each launch team member.

Let the community know you're launching a new church site.

- *Volunteers are scheduled and trained.* At a minimum, you should have a hospitality team, kids team, and media team for the first service. They should know their roles well.
- *Signage is visible and clear.* Having good signage does two things: (1) It shows people that you are expecting them, and (2) it makes people feel more comfortable because they know where to go.
- *Serve coffee—but not bad coffee.* Just because you can save a few dollars with less-expensive coffee doesn't mean you should. Make sure you serve good coffee (and some refreshments). When people gather to eat and drink, it fosters the building of relationships.
- *The building is clean.* Sweep. Mop. Take out the trash. Make the building look clean. Parents of young kids will notice if it's not clean.
- *Have the right amount of seating.* You don't want to run out of seats. At the same time, you don't want to have so many seats that the worship space feels empty. More people will come to the launch service than the preview services. You can easily have double the number of people at launch compared to the previews.
- *Have a well-planned, well-executed worship service.* Plan out an order of service. Make sure the length of time is good. Outline all the speaking parts. Create smooth transitions.
- *The worship team (and preacher) at launch is the same team that leads the next week.* The launch service should resemble what will happen every week. If the week following the launch is dramatically different, people won't come back.

- *The message is prepared and prayed over.* The Launch Sunday sermon should never be a "Saturday Night Special."
- *You are prepared for children.* Is your kids ministry prepared? Are rooms set up and cleaned? Have you thought through the check-in and checkout process? If you do not have a kids ministry, are you providing activity packs for kids in the worship service?
- *First-time guests leave with something in their hands.* I recommend providing gifts (e.g., coffee mugs, stickers, pens) to all first-time guests. There is something out there for all budgets.
- *You collect information from attendees.* During the service, ask everyone to fill out an information card or connection card. At my church, we donate five dollars to local ministries for every card turned in. It motivates people to provide their information. Make sure you follow up!
- *You collect an offering.* If you plan to do this weekly, make sure you do it on Launch Sunday.
- *You count how many people attend.* Make sure you distinguish between guests you know are not coming back (e.g., out-of-towners) and those who could become regular attenders.
- *You build relationships.* Don't get caught up in the logistics of Launch Sunday and fail to meet people.

Did you notice what I didn't include as part of a successful launch? Numbers. You want to count how many people attend, but a successful Launch Sunday doesn't have to have a numerical goal. It's not wrong to have a goal, but it's not necessary for success. The median size church in the United States is seventy-five people.[1] Not every church can (or should) be a megachurch. But every church can be intentional about reaching its community. If you focus on reaching and retaining people, growth will come.

You Are Launching More than a Worship Service

Starting a new church site primarily focuses on two things: (1) gathering people and (2) Launch Sunday. But you are launching a lot more than just a worship service. Don't get so focused on your first worship service that you fail to start a church.

What does the launch *of a church* look like at the beginning? I believe it's better to do a few things with excellence than to do many things with mediocrity. You only get one chance to make a good first impression as a church in your community. Focus on doing a few ministries well. Your priority should be to establish the ministries associated with the worship service.

1. Prayer
2. Worship/preaching
3. Small groups
4. Kids ministry
5. Welcome and hospitality

To be clear, this doesn't mean you can't develop other aspects of ministry. You want to establish and maintain an outward focus right from the beginning, building on the community relationships you have developed during the start-up process. When I refer to these first five ministries, I call them *formalized* ministries. Each one should have a dedicated leader, with accountability. This can include a mixture of full-time, part-time, and volunteer roles. And one person can oversee more than one ministry.

It will be tempting to try to do more at the very beginning. A common fear among many leaders of new churches is that "people won't stay if we don't provide enough things to do." That might be true. A new church isn't for everyone. If people are looking for lots of big programs and ministries, an established church may be a better fit for them. You're not launching a fifty-year-old church. A new church is about having a big vision for reaching new people.

A phrase I often used during the first few years of our church plants is that "we will act our age." When we were new and young, we only attempted to do what we could do, but we learned and grew quickly. We crawled when we could crawl. We walked when we were able to walk. And we ran when we were able to run.

When Do You Start Adding Ministries?

As the church grows, you will need to evaluate which ministries to formalize next. Let the growth of the church determine your direction here. Let the vision statement guide what you do next. Most important, let God lead and define the church's next steps.

Below is a suggested timeline for which ministries to formalize when. Depending on your context, you can add ministries or remove them from the list.

Within the first three months
Develop your finance team
Develop your assimilation team

Within the first six months
Develop your administrative team
Develop your communications teams

Within the first twelve months

Develop your student ministry

Develop your missions team

Develop your facilities team

No matter which ministries you add after your launch and when, there is one thing you will always need: *leaders*.

Invest Time in Leadership Development

The biggest obstacle to starting any ministry is leadership. There always is more ministry available than people to lead.

Remember the hiring pipeline from chapter 4?

Paid Volunteer	→	Contract Worker	→	Part-Time Staff	→	Full-Time Staff

If you have paid volunteers, there's a good chance they are leading one or two ministries in your new church. The hard part isn't paying your volunteers. The hard part is developing a paid volunteer into a leader.

There's a lot of information available about leadership development. The goal for a new church leader is not to become an expert on the subject. The goal is to have some form of leadership development in place. The key is to be intentional about developing leaders. Create a simple process or pipeline.

Here's a simple leadership pipeline for a new church:

Unpaid Volunteer	→	Leader of Volunteers	→	Leader of Leaders	→	Paid Volunteer

Leadership development can feel overwhelming at first. The easiest way to start developing leaders is by starting with *one*. Choose a likely candidate from your launch team and start investing your time. Teach him or her how to move from volunteering to leadership, and what it means to lead others. Think about what *you* do as a leader. Write it all down on a sheet of paper. Let your leader-in-training watch you lead. Then flip the script. Let him or her lead while you observe. Once a person knows how to lead others, he or she can be taught how to develop new leaders. That's all it means to be a leader of leaders.

Leadership development boiled down to its simplest form looks like this:

I do. You watch.

You do. I watch.

Be intentional about developing new leaders. The launch of a new church is the beginning of reaching new people and training new leaders.

Are you ready to launch? The answer is not about having everything in place for Launch Sunday. That's important, but it's not the answer to the question.

You are ready to launch when you are prepared to lead the new church for the next twelve months (and beyond). Establishing a new church is more than just an event. Launching a new church is about long-term Kingdom work. When you are ready to launch into a new season of ministry, you are prepared to launch a new church site.

10

Ready for Change?

THE CHURCH YOU START TODAY will not be the same church you lead in the future.

New churches change. Most new churches change a lot. Planning and envisioning a future for your new church is important; holding those future plans loosely is even more important. The variables in a new church start-up are endless. Pastor Ed Stetzer once told me that starting a new church is "constantly solving a series of crises." He was right. The time I spent planting a church with him taught me how quickly ministry changes and how quickly leaders must respond to change.

The question is not, "Will change occur?" The question is, "Are you ready for the change that will occur?"

What Will Change?

My first inclination is to write "everything" and move on to the next section. That might be helpful for some, but not for everyone. Here's a brief list of what will likely change in your new church:

- *People:* You probably already assumed this one. There isn't just a front door and a back door in a new church. It's more like a *revolving* door! It can feel as if people leave as quickly as they come in. But remember that God brings specific people at specific times for specific purposes to start a church.
- *Ministries:* Your new church will always have specific ministries. Some ministries may come and go. But how you lead and implement the ministries will change over the first few years.
- *Church systems:* You'll find or develop new and better systems as the church grows.
- *Staff and volunteers:* When my current church first started, I was the youngest person on the team. Six years later, I'm the oldest. While I didn't set out to change the demographics of the staff, it goes to show how quickly things can change in a new church site.
- *Leadership:* Depending on the structure and governance of your new church, your top leadership will change. Elders and deacons will change. Directors and leaders will change. Providing stability among the church's leadership is essential. Communicate leadership changes in advance. Plan ahead if possible. Too much change in leadership for a new church can create some unwanted ripples.

- *Location/building:* It's unusual for a new church to find its "forever home" in the first few years. You may want to assess your growth pattern and potential before deciding on a permanent location. Ideally, though, you will stay within the community where you first launched.
- *Vision, mission, strategy, and culture:* Your strategies should change every two years or so to adapt to changes in your community and your church and to keep things fresh. Your vision and mission might change as well, but be strategic about how, when, and why you change them.
- *Outreach methods:* How you reach people should continually be changing because you are continually finding new people to reach. Don't let your evangelism and outreach become stagnant.
- *The name of the church:* Hold all plans loosely! You never know what God might be up to.

Don't be fearful of what will change. Just be prepared. And don't try to stop change as it happens. As soon as you stand still, you start slipping backward. A new church needs to grow, and with growth comes change. To stifle change is to stifle growth.

The Four Different Churches You Will Lead in the First Five Years

The church you start today will not be the same church you lead in the future. Having been part of three new church plants over the past ten years, I've noticed a pattern of how new churches change. There's a good chance you will lead four (or more) different churches—all within the church you launched—within the first five years!

About eighteen months after launching my current church, I remember looking out into the congregation while preaching and thinking, *I barely know these people*. Now some of the originals were tried and true, but a new group of people had entered into the life of our church and the culture had changed slightly as a result. Each cycle of a new church will bring in different cultures. That's why it's so important to define and live out the church's culture from the very beginning. So, what's the pattern of change in a new church?

The "Shiny Object" Church

In most contexts, a new church is attractive. Words such as *new*, *start-up*, and *plant* will draw people in naturally. But who does a new church attract? I've found that new churches typically attract a mixture of dechurched and churched.

Attracting the dechurched is a good thing. For clarity, the dechurched are those who used to attend a church but stopped. This group may have been out of church for years. The dechurched come to new churches hoping they can get a fresh start. Make your new church a place where the formerly churched can reignite their relationship with Jesus.

New churches also attract the churched—people who currently attend another church but may be unhappy there. I encourage you to resist transfer growth from the beginning. The rare exception would be when someone feels called to help launch a new church. These people usually show up during the pre-launch season, not after the church launches.

Starting a new church isn't about making a place for the churched; it's about reaching the unchurched and drawing back the dechurched. It's about reaching people who are far from Christ and showing them the hope that is in Christ. The start-up season only happens once. Make the most of it for God's glory. All shiny things fade over time. No matter what, stay focused on your vision, mission, strategy, and culture. There's danger looming if you don't.

The "My Way" Church

Around the one-year mark at my current church, our culture shifted. For the previous twenty-four months (twelve months of pre-launch and twelve months of post-launch), we had focused on reaching people who were far from Christ. But now it seemed I was spending less time sharing Christ with the unchurched and more time resolving conflicts among the church members. The conflicts started small—usually over silly things such as where to store the supplies in the church building. Then the conflicts began to grow into more significant issues. Personal conflict was on the rise. Leadership teams were starting to not see eye-to-eye. What changed?

The "shiny object" church had lost its shine. In addition, there was no longer a strong emphasis on the church's vision and mission. Though I don't think it happened intentionally, people started wanting things done "their way" in the church. We moved from a culture of ownership and empowerment to one of control. Ownership and empowerment can be good. Grasping for control is never good. Now I was leading a church with many people who wanted control over certain aspects of the church.

I had many difficult conversations over the next twelve months. The more time I spent resolving conflict, the less time I spent leading the church and reaching the unchurched. During this season, well-intentioned families left. And some of the ill-intentioned families stayed. I knew things had to change.

Around the two-and-a-half-year mark, some of the top leaders left the church. Though it was hard to see them go, it created an opportunity. I immediately brought in some new leaders, cast a new vision for the church, and asked some families if they might be happier in another church. Again, it was hard, but sometimes you need to tell someone, "Maybe this isn't the church for you." The other families that wanted the church to operate "their way" soon left on their own. The families that remained were committed to the vision of the church.

The "Committed" Church

The influx of new leadership and our revitalized vision reignited the church. We went back to our original focus: being a Great Commission and Great Commandment church.[1] Though the newness had worn off, the church overcame the season of conflict. Our people were now more committed than ever. It was easy to lead during this season because the people in the church were committed to doing whatever it took to advance God's Kingdom.

We used this time to grow the foundation of the church. We saw an increase in our finances, attendance, small group participation, leadership development, and baptisms. The growth wasn't exponential, but it was consistent. During this season, we also purchased a permanent facility. Our roots were growing deeper and stronger in the community. I could tell our church was ready to move in some significant ways.

Then the global pandemic hit. As with every other church, it affected ours in several ways: We paused our on-site worship services, the number of volunteers decreased, and our ministry became largely digital. But even through the lockdowns and quarantines, our church stayed committed. When a sense of normalcy began to return, our congregation came back hungry. They were ready to do something.

The "Ready to Do Something" Church

The pandemic only delayed what our church would do next. Our core was committed and ready for something big. Our vision was big. Our strategy was big. Our efforts were extensive. The year after the pandemic, we had the most baptisms in a single year we had ever seen. This "ready for action" attitude and demeanor carried over into the following year as well.

Your new church site will change over the first five years. With the Holy Spirit's guidance, lead the change. Be proactive in prayer and ready to respond to the Spirit's prompting. Build deeper relationships in each phase. And no matter what change comes your way, remember that God is in control.

Don't Lose Focus

I've said it throughout the chapter, but I want to make it clear. Keep your focus on the God-given vision and the mission of your new church. Even if you change your church's vision or mission along the way, keep it as your priority. Change is easier when you know where you're going. If you lose focus along the way, change can be unnecessary and painful.

Are you ready for change? If you stay focused on your vision and dependent on the Holy Spirit's guidance, you'll be ready for change. Let God make changes for his Kingdom and his glory.

Conclusion

A New Church Site Is Only the Beginning

As MUCH AS LAUNCHING a new church feels like a finish line, it's not. It's only the beginning of the race. All the work you did to prepare for the launch was also to prepare you for the race ahead. To put it more accurately, all the work you did to prepare for the launch was to *build the racecourse* and prepare you for the race. You may be tempted to take a break right after you launch the new site. Don't. That would be the equivalent of sitting down at the starting line after completing your stretches. The next phase in the life of your new church will be critical. Now is the time to run.

Find Your Pace

Long-distance runners know their pace. As soon as the race starts, they get into their stride and find their pace. Taking off too fast will tire them out too quickly. Taking off too slowly will put them behind where they need to be for the long haul.

You need to set the proper pace for your new church. Find a sustainable stride for the road ahead. A new church is fragile. Getting into healthy rhythms as soon as possible moves the church from fragility to stability. How do you find your stride as a new church? Here are three ways:

Celebrate Anything and Everything

Remember the tried-and-true leadership principle mentioned in chapter 3 that says, "What gets celebrated gets replicated"? Celebrate anything that reinforces your vision, mission, strategy, and culture as a new church. If someone invites a new person to church, celebrate it. If someone takes out the trash without being asked, celebrate it. Celebrate if someone takes a first-time guest out to lunch after church. If a child memorizes a Bible verse, celebrate it. If an adult memorizes a Bible verse, celebrate it!

I think you get the point. Look for reasons to celebrate the small and big wins in your new church. It matters to people and makes a big difference in how they view their involvement. For at least the first few years in the life of the new church, throw big "church birthday" parties. Make every baptism a cause for celebration. As you celebrate the wins, they will be replicated throughout the church. As more people replicate the church's vision and mission, the pace will not only become more steady, it will even increase.

Move from a Launch Team to a Leadership Team

Now that the church has launched, it's time to disband and decommission the launch team. Their work is done. Now is the time to create a leadership team if you haven't already. But be careful to put the right people on the team. Look for people who are carrying out the functions of a leadership role even without the title. It's easy to ask people to take on other functions; it's not so easy to change someone's title. Even if your initial team is small, establishing a leadership team will build stability. People will know who to look to. The leadership team can help support and reinforce the vision and mission.

Move People from Attenders to Members

Much like the benefits of establishing a leadership team, moving people from attenders to members will create stability. It also adds accountability and responsibility. People who commit to membership should feel some of the weight of accomplishing the vision and mission of the church. Giving members responsibility and accountability will increase the pace of the church's progress.

Find your pace. Then look at the road ahead.

Visualize the Race

Launching a new church site is a time for dreaming. Church planters are constantly looking to the future and imagining the possibilities. But it's amazing how quickly that mindset can disappear after launch day, when the daily grind of ministry sets in. Church leaders stop looking for the next mile marker and start focusing on the cracks and the rocks in the road right in front of them.

Please hear me clearly on this: *Don't stop dreaming!* At the very least, take several hours one day per month to visualize where God might be leading your church. Ask yourself a series of questions:

- What happens if the church doubles in size in the next year?
- What would we do if our budget increased by 50 percent?
- How could our church reach the community in ways that no other church has ever done?
- What if every person in our church were in a disciple-making relationship?
- What if every person in our church shared the gospel at least once a year?
- How could our church start a second worship service?
- How could our church develop the most dynamic kids and student ministries?

There is a question I have kept at the forefront of my mind over the years of planting three churches: *Would our community notice or care if we closed the church's doors for good?*

I encourage you to think through your answer to that question. I also encourage you to dream about a church that would have such a positive and substantial impact on the community that people would grieve if the church shut down. Dream on that idea for a while.

What would it take for your church to have such an influence on the community that everyone would agree that the church must stay open? Visualize that kind of church. Dream about that kind of church. And keep running toward your vision of that church.

Teach Someone Else to Run

As I said at the outset, we need more churches. Now that you've started a new church, you have a gift. It's not a gift to keep, but a gift to give away. You have the gift of knowing how to start a new church. That is a gift you can share time and again.

Get someone from the crowd to join you in the race. Intentionally train up another new church leader who will start a new church. Why? Because we need more churches! The sooner you teach someone else to run this race, the sooner your new church will be ready to launch another new church. If possible, find a future new church leader from the very beginning of your own church site launch process. Learn the process together as you launch your new church site. After your new church has launched, the new church leader can start the process again.

The longer you wait to start another new church, the less likely it will happen. If possible, start another new church within the first five years. Even better, start within the first three years. Find new church leaders and committed church members who will support the new initiative. Train them up and send them out.

Give God Glory

There is one Bible verse that I have consistently read, prayed, recited, and preached over the years of starting new churches:

> Now all glory to God, who is able, through his mighty power at work within us, to accomplish infinitely more than we might ask or think. Glory to him in the church and in Christ Jesus through all generations forever and ever! Amen.
>
> EPHESIANS 3:20-21

As leaders and members of new churches, we are simply conduits for God to work through. God will use his mighty power to accomplish his will through us. As leaders and committed members of new churches, we must allow God's power and purpose to flow. Don't get in the way. When we are conduits for God's purpose and power, he will accomplish more through us than we could ever imagine. Let him work. Let him work in you. Let him work through you.

In everything, give God the glory. Let God's glory be known no matter what happens in your new church. Praise his name to your neighbors and to the nations. He is our hope and our future. He is the reason we live. To him be all the glory.

Notes

INTRODUCTION: WE NEED MORE CHURCHES

1. Michael Lipka, "A Closer Look at America's Rapidly Growing Religious 'Nones,'" Pew Research Center, May 13, 2015, https://www.pewresearch.org/fact-tank/2015/05/13/a-closer-look-at-americas-rapidly-growing-religious-nones; Jana Riess, "The 'Nones' Are Growing—and Growing More Diverse," Religion News Service, March 24, 2021, https://religionnews.com/2021/03/24/the-nones-are-growing-and-growing-more-diverse.

2. Chuck Lawless, "8 Reasons Churches Don't Do Evangelism Well," blog, June 18, 2020, https://chucklawless.com/2020/06/8-reasons-churches-dont-do-evangelism-well.

3. C. Peter Wagner, *Church Planting for a Greater Harvest* (Ventura, CA: Regal, 1990), 11.

CHAPTER 1: ARE YOU SURE YOU WANT TO DO THIS?

1. Aubrey Malphurs, *The Nuts and Bolts of Church Planting: A Guide for Starting Any Kind of Church* (Grand Rapids, MI: Baker, 2011), 9.

2. Malphurs, *Nuts and Bolts of Church Planting*, 9.

CHAPTER 2: WHAT WILL YOUR CHURCH SITE LOOK LIKE?

1. Thom S. Rainer, "Five Reasons Why Church Adoption and Church Fostering Are Such Important Movements," Church Answers blog, August 24, 2020, https://churchanswers.com/blog/five-reasons-why-church-adoption-and-church-fostering-are-such-important-movements.

2. Rainer, "Five Reasons Why."

3. A useful tool for this process is the Know Your Community report from Church Answers. See https://churchanswers.com/solutions/tools/kyc/know-your-community.

4. See, for example, Church on Wheels (www.churchonwheels.com).

CHAPTER 3: DO YOU HAVE VISION?

1. See, for example, https://www.99designs.com.

CHAPTER 4: WHO WILL BE ON THE TEAM?

1. See Eric Geiger, "Character First, But Is Chemistry or Competence Next?" blog, September 24, 2019, https://ericgeiger.com/2019/09/character-first-but-is-chemistry-or-competence-next; Greg Henderson, "The Three C's of Leadership," *Forbes*, December 30, 2021, https://www.forbes.com/sites/forbeshumanresourcescouncil/2021/12/30/the-three-cs-of-leadership/?sh=22ff4214f1bc; Paul Comfort, "Does Character Matter? The Three C's of Leadership," business.com, June 29, 2022, https://www.business.com/articles/the-three-cs-of-leadership.
2. I first read about the role of paid volunteers in Nelson Searcy and Kerrick Thomas, *Launch: Starting a New Church from Scratch* (Ventura, CA: Regal, 2017).

CHAPTER 6: WHAT'S UNDER THE HOOD?

1. I recommend QuickBooks Online (https://quickbooks.intuit.com).
2. I have used Church Community Builder and Realm/ACS in the past.
3. See, for example, www.wix.com or www.squarespace.com.
4. I currently use www.Ekklesia360.com.
5. See "Worldwide Desktop Market Share of Leading Search Engines from January 2010 to January 2022, Statista, accessed June 30, 2022, https://www.statista.com/statistics/216573/worldwide-market-share-of-search-engines/.

CHAPTER 7: WHERE ARE THE PEOPLE?

1. Nelson Searcy and Kerrick Thomas, *Launch: Starting a New Church from Scratch* (Ventura, CA: Regal, 2017), 142.
2. Sam Rainer, "A Few Surprising Perspectives about Your Unchurched Neighbors," Church Answers blog, July 21, 2021, https://churchanswers.com/blog/a-few-surprising-perspectives-about-your-unchurched-neighbors.

CHAPTER 9: READY TO LAUNCH?

1. Sam Rainer, "What Two Simple Statistics Reveal about the American Church," Sam Rainer blog, January 21, 2018, https://samrainer.com/2018/01/what-two-simple-statistics-reveal-about-the-american-church.

CHAPTER 10: READY FOR CHANGE?

1. Pastor J. T. English offers the following insights: "The Great Commission will be fulfilled by Great Commandment Christians. To be a Great Commandment Christian is to love God with your whole self and to love your neighbor. The Great Commission is to create Great Commandment Christians. The Great Commandment invites us to participate in the Great Commission, and the Great Commission invites us to participate in the Great Commandment." See J. T. English, *Deep Discipleship: How the Church Can Make Whole Disciples of Jesus* (Nashville, TN: B&H, 2020), 161–162.

About the Author

JESS RAINER is lead pastor for The Church at Spring Hill, a church plant in a suburb of Nashville. He is a cofounder of Rainer Publishing and the founder and owner of Craft Book Publishing. He also coauthored *The Millennials: Connecting to America's Largest Generation.*

Jess received a BS in finance from Murray State University and an MA in Christian education from Southeastern Seminary. Jess is married to the love of his life, Rachel, and they have four children: Canon, Will (now with the Lord), Harper, and Collins.

If you liked this book, you'll want to get involved in

Church Equip!

—

Do you have a desire to learn more about serving God through your local church?

Would you like to see how God can use you in new and exciting ways?

Get your church involved in Church Equip, an online ministry designed to prepare church leaders and church members to better serve God's mission and purpose.

Check us out at **ChurchEquip.com**